CW00695627

About the Author

D.U. Sivri is a qualified psychotherapist who has spent years working on and developing his unique eclectic brand of counselling and therapy. Having spent many years living and working in a number of countries, he has adapted ideologies and techniques from many different cultures to bring you the secrets of existence and fulfilment.

Dedication

To my father whose advice, intelligence, kindness and humour is greatly missed, and to Michelle whose love, support and belief made this book possible.

D. U. SIVRI

THE SECRETS OF EXISTENCE AND FULFILMENT

AUSTIN MACAULEY
PUBLISHERS LTD.

A CIP catalogue record for this title is available from the British Library.

The information in this book is intended to be educational, and should not be misused in any way whatsoever. The information, although diagnostic by nature, should not replace consultation with a qualified healthcare professional. The content of this book is intended to be used as an adjunct to a rational, responsible and qualified healthcare programme. The author and publisher are in no way liable for any misuse of the content.

ISBN 978 1 78455 681 5 (Paperback)
ISBN 978 1 78455 683 9 (Hardback)

www.austinmacauley.com

First Published (2015)
Austin Macauley Publishers Ltd.
25 Canada Square
Canary Wharf
London
E14 5LB

Printed and bound in Great Britain

Acknowledgments

Thank you to my family and friends for making this book become a reality. Thank you to all the people I have helped over the years…by helping you, I have also helped myself.

CONTENTS

INTRODUCTION

We all need help at various points in our lives. Work can be challenging, boring and repetitive. Our relationships can be difficult, unfulfilling and problematic. Family life can be monotone, humdrum and un-inspiring …

So what is it that separates certain people from others? Why is it that some people can get through life and make a success of everything, and others seem to be stuck in a perpetual rut of negativity and underachievement? Is there a 'magic formula' that enables some people to always 'come up smelling of roses', whilst for others life tends to be one long struggle …

My years working as a psychotherapist have meant that I have encountered people from all walks of life and have helped them to deal with all types of problems in their daily lives. For the majority of people, their lives just need 'tweaking', certain readjustments and improvements on a practical level to help them move forwards in life. For others, the solutions are more complex, they involve deeper psychological questions that need to be addressed and answers that need to be found in relation to their perceptions and understanding of their lives.

We all have similar issues in life, but what defines some people from others is their ability to cope with certain adverse situations in their lives and use those definitive points to their advantage, rather than to their detriment.

After all, who hasn't worried about the following things:

Aging

Being Alone

Losing a Loved One

Relationships Ending

Intimacy

Change

Being Assertive

Having Enough Money

Health

Being Successful

Death

We have all worried about some, if not all of the above, at various points in our lives. Maybe you could add a few more to the list of things that worry you.

Whatever has affected you adversely in your life, this book will give you the insight and tools to be pro-active, helping you to vastly improve your ability to deal with any given situation.

What I have endeavored to get across in my work, is that in most cases, it's not a psychological problem people suffer from, per se, but it's more a question of being able to 're-define' and 're-educate' the mind. I have spent hours talking to people and sending emails, where I have tried to reassure people that whenever they feel hopeless or stuck in a rut, the solutions aren't always as difficult as they envisage.

Sometimes it's just a question of being *mindful*, of recognizing what you are thinking and challenging those 'little voices' of negativity that keep popping up every time you want to say or do something. I will help you to drown out those negative voices that have held you back in life. Sometimes it can take an *Epiphany* to force you to change, and at other times, it's just a question of working with yourself and diligence that enable you to get the results you are looking for. Whatever we do to make us change, the reality is that we must do *something!* "If we do what we have always done, we will get what we have always gotten" is the old adage… And when it comes to our lives, this is very true.

We tend to think that the answers to our problems lie somewhere else. In reality all the solutions to our difficulties lie within us. We just have to learn how to unlock the potential that we have and use it to enhance and benefit our lives. Of course, sometimes we need a Guide, a Coach or a Mentor to point us in the right direction. That's where someone like me comes along. I have spent years helping people realise their true potential. I have met people from ALL walks of life:

Actors, Singers, Sportsmen and Sportswomen, City Highfliers, Lawyers, Housewives, Blue-Collar Workers, Couples, Singles, you name it … I've met them all! Whatever their jobs or backgrounds, they all have one thing in common:

The Desire to Improve their Lives

Sometimes it's THAT simple. It starts with a desire. Then becomes an uncontrollable quest to find answers to improve their lives or to find a deeper meaning to *what it's all about*.

Sometimes it is Fear that drives us, other times it is Love, and once in a while we are driven by a force that even we don't truly understand. What I have found though, is that, whatever the reason is for change, we can't always fight it. It has a power all of its own that remains un-satiated until it is accomplished.

Change is inevitable. It is nothing to worry about or be fearful of. That is why you have bought this book in the first place: You already KNOW you need to change for the better. Maybe you have procrastinated, or maybe you have put it off because you have been too busy, or fearful, but whatever your excuses have been, you know that NOW is the time for that change to happen.

Changing our lives for the better is not easy, but together we will look at:

* Ways to experience more joy in your life

* Ways to give your life more purpose and meaning

* Ways to make your hopes and wishes become reality

* Ways to become more assertive

* Ways to improve self-confidence

* Ways to re-programme your thought patterns

* Ways to deal with negative people in your life

* Ways to understand you are responsible for your life

* Ways to find Inner Peace

* Ways to find more satisfaction, love and trust in your life

* Ways to be more sympathetic and empathetic

* Ways to better understand yourself and others

* Ways to overcome your fears and live your life more optimally

Of course, some areas of self-improvement may relate to you more than others. The key is to focus on the areas that you need to work more on, yet at the same time incorporate all the areas into your life so that you feel improved in all aspects of your day-to-day living. Sometimes, things work with a knock-on effect; once you knock over the first domino, they will all topple over. Improving yourself is like that. Once you improve a certain area of your life, then the benefits can also be observed in other areas. Improvements will follow on naturally.

No matter what area of your life and to what level you want to empower and improve yourself, NOW is the perfect time to shake off the shackles of procrastination. Together we can look at and work on certain aspects of your life, but ultimately, *you* have the potential and power to be the person you deserve to be.

I will also present you with case studies so you can see other people in similar situations to the ones you find yourself in, and the solutions they found to overcoming any debilitating factors in their lives. I will also give you the psychological tools you will need to enhance your life and provide you with relevant definitions and quotes to help you understand and implement new ideas and new ways of thinking.

Everything you read in this book is based on facts and knowledge I have gained over the years working as a psychotherapist using Cognitive – Behavioral Therapy and an eclectic mix of other schools of psychological thought.

Finally, I would like to thank you for reading *The Secrets of Existence and Fulfilment*, and I would like to congratulate you in finding the courage to take the first steps forward in becoming a better and more contented *You*.

CHAPTER ONE:

FACING YOUR FEARS

"**Fear.** n. **1** an unpleasant emotion caused by the threat of danger, pain or harm. **2** the likelihood of something unwelcome happening. **v. 1** be afraid of. **2** (**fear for**) be anxious about."

- ORIGIN Old English, 'danger'

Oxford English Dictionary

Who hasn't felt fear at some point in his or her life? Either real fear or perceived fear. In fact, for every single one of us working in the psychology sector, *perceived fear* is what we work with most of the time. Most of our clients are fearful of something terrible that will happen to them. They seem to have an *innate* sense of foreboding that for some reason, leaves them feeling paralyzed when it comes to dealing with what they fear the most. The reality is that their minds take over and as this happens, the physiological effects on their bodies (release of hormones, heavy breathing, sweaty palms, etc.) result in the mental processes actually becoming physical. So what starts in the mind, manifests itself in the body. Whether these fears are real or not, the results on the body to all intents and purposes are the same. For these people their fears then become very real on every level.

So what is it that people can be fearful of?

Let's look at a few case studies and see if you recognize any of your fears in the following scenarios …

* Dana is thirty-eight years old. She has a good job in London, is married, has a young daughter and lives in a nice part of town. From the outside, her life looks fairly idyllic and trouble free. So what is it that Dana is fearful of?

"Every day I wake up and I'm worried that I'm just not good enough. My job is so demanding and draining, that I fear I will have a breakdown. I am worried that I'm not a good mother. I don't have any maternal feelings towards my child and I'm scared that I might damage her psychologically in some way. My life is not fulfilling me at all. I don't think I love my husband and I'm fearful that the marriage is not satisfying me the way I had hoped it would. I feel trapped, lonely and desperate and most of the time I am scared that I may do something that I regret. I'm constantly on edge and I can't see a way forwards. Also, on top of everything, my family live abroad and I constantly worry about them too. I'm scared of losing my job, my marriage and my sanity …"

Dana's life is racked with fear. She is worried and fearful in every situation in her life. Can you relate to any of the fears she has? Here are some more examples:

* Margaret is sixty-five years old. She is a financial expert in an international company in The City of London. She has worked hard all her life and is extremely well respected and admired in her field. She has many clients, a very good salary, an apartment in the centre of London and a country house. What could Margaret possibly be fearful of?

"I have been a workaholic all my life. I have worked long hours every day and have strived for perfection in what I do. I live for my job and can't see a life away from my work. I have pushed myself to be successful, despite my fear of being around people. I dislike public speaking and meetings… I feel as if I'm always being judged by everyone. I decided a long time ago that I didn't want children, which I now deeply regret. In reality, my family is my job and workplace. My husband is very tolerant of me, but I'm scared that deep down, my home life may not be stimulating enough for me… I have decided to retire, but I just can't bring myself to cut back on work. I dread the idea of stopping work altogether. What will I do if I stop? How will I occupy those empty hours? Retirement fills me with dread and fear for the future. What if I get depressed, how will I cope then? Will my husband still be as supportive as he is now?"

Margaret's future seems like a void filled with emptiness, hopelessness and fear. When you think of your future, do any of her fears resonate with you?

* Michael is forty-one years old, lives and works in London, and he is a manager at a financial firm. He is successful, hard-working and diligent. He has just bought a new apartment and is looking forward to the next phase of his life. What could Michael possibly be scared of?

"My biggest fear is being single for the rest of my life. I have been in a few relationships but they just haven't worked out for me. Maybe I make the wrong choices … Also, I am gay; that's not a problem in itself, but I didn't 'come out' until I was in my early thirties. I even had a few relationships with girls in my twenties. I was so confused when I was younger. I felt I needed to do the right thing for my family and friends. At that time, that meant finding a nice girl and settling down. I wasn't really being true to myself. If I could turn back the clock, I would have done things differently. Maybe if I had, my life would have turned out differently. I wouldn't have made all the bad choices that I did make. The worst thing is that there is no-one out there for me … I truly believe that. Nothing will make me see things differently. I don't believe that anyone can love me, and I don't believe that I have a soul-mate out there. I am scared of ending up alone. I wish things had been different. Why can't I find love and be in a normal relationship like other people are …?"

Have you ever felt as alone as Michael has? Have you ever wondered if there was someone out there in the world for you the same way that he has? Have you ever been fearful that you would end up old and lonely, and all by yourself?

Before we look at some more case studies, let us take a more in depth look at what *Fear* is, with a more psychological definition, together with techniques and tools to overcome its debilitating effects.

Fear An emotional state in the presence or anticipation of a dangerous or noxious stimulus. Fear is usually characterized by an internal, subjective experience of extreme agitation, a desire to flee or to attack, and a variety of sympathetic reactions. Fear is often differentiated from Anxiety on one (or both) of two grounds:

(a) Fear is treated as involving specific objects or events while anxiety is regarded as a more general emotional state;

(b) Fear is considered a reaction to a present danger, anxiety to an anticipated or imagined one.

(Also Phobia, a specific, persistent, irrational fear).

Dictionary of Psychology, Penguin Reference

So how can we counter all this? What can we do as individuals to help ourselves when we have these intrusive and debilitating thoughts? What are the measures we can take to re-define and re-educate our minds?

Well, once you become aware of your negative thinking which leads to a particular emotional disturbance, be it worry, anxiety or fear, you can learn to modify your thinking by looking at the following psychological procedures:

1. Learn to see that your *Beliefs* lead to emotional and behavioral *Consequences*.

2. Check that you have a strong motivation to *change* your emotional disturbances and behaviors when you realize the *Consequences*.

3. Realize that thinking in a more realistic way regarding your *Beliefs* will lead to a reduction in disturbed emotions/ behaviors at the *Consequence* stage.

4. Focus on weighing up the evidence for and against your *Beliefs*.

5. Focus on generating more realistic alternatives to your *Beliefs*.

In the above model, **Beliefs** can be defined in the psychological sense as a feeling and emotional acceptance that something exists or is true (especially one without proof).These acceptances can relate to deeply held perceptions, ideas or doctrines.

Consequences can be defined as, the results, conclusions or effects of a certain phenomenon which were brought on by a series of precipitating events or factors.

There are three main categories of strategies to modify your negative thoughts and thinking in the above procedures:

- Verbal (Use of words)

- Imaginal (Use of images)

- Behavioral (Use of actions)

In the same way you can evaluate and test a scientific hypothesis, a Belief can be verified by evaluating the available evidence relating to that Belief. Evidence concerning the validity of your Belief can be obtained from your knowledge and previous experiences (your verbal and imaginal disputing) or by a means of a behavioral check list (behavioral disputing). These strategies can be used to challenge your *inferences* about what has happened in a situation, or to challenge your *evaluations* about what has happened.

(*Inferences* – acts or processes of deriving logical conclusions from premises known or assumed to be true.

Evaluations – systematic determinations of a subject's merit, worth and significance, using criteria governed by a set of standards).

Verbal Methods of Modifying Your Negative/ Fearful Behaviour

Question Yourself

Any negative or maladaptive thoughts you may have can be challenged by the most useful tool to use; Questions. Rather than trying to find useful or realistic alternatives for your negative thoughts or fears, it is far better to elicit realistic thinking by means of questioning.

Where possible, try to avoid using 'why' questions as these may be more difficult for you to answer (though not impossible!). Try to use 'how', 'what' and 'who' questions as you may find these more productive. Below you'll find some types of questions that will help you when you learn to start disputing your negative and fearful thoughts.

'What is the evidence that …?'

'How can I find out more about …?'

'What makes that so bad for me?'

'How does it follow that …?'

'Who can give me the information that I need?'

'And if that were the case?'

'What is the very worst thing that could happen …?'

'Who says I must?'

'How does that mean that …?'

'What would it take to convince me that …?'

'What does it say about me if …?'

'Is that something that I really want or need?'

'Is there any proof that …?'

So for example, if we take the first question: 'What is the evidence that …?'

When you are fearful, negative thinking starts to take over and your mind starts wandering and all your thoughts are geared towards past wrongs or past hurts; the negativity leads you to start thinking in ways you don't want to and you may start doing things that could be perceived as being *paranoid*. At this point, you should start using the questioning process.

Example:-

If you have been cheated on in the past, then you may be pre-disposed to thinking your partners are likely to cheat on you. After all, the *seed has been sown,* and you then find yourself looking for the *water* (the evidence) to feed your doubts and fears.

Questioning Process

"What is the evidence that my partner is cheating?"

Ask the question, then look for the evidence.

Then continue in this manner …

"Is there any proof that my partner is unfaithful?"

Ask the question, then look for any proof.

"What would it take to convince me that my partner loves me?"

Ask the question and find the confirmation that you need.

You can continue with as many types of questions that you need in order to find *Real Answers* instead of letting your imagination run riot.

In addition to questioning, there are a few other strategies that you can use to help you evaluate the evidence regarding your fearful beliefs and the rationality of your negative thinking. These strategies include:

- Information – Gaining

- Use of Comparisons

- Use of Humor

- Role Models (Modelling)

- Role Playing

Information – Gaining

Knowledge and information can be very important for you when you have a misconception about your worries and fears. For example, if you have panic disorders, are overly fearful, or are generally anxious, you may develop negative physical symptoms that you believe support your state of distress and angst (Psychosomatic – physical illnesses caused by mental factors). Gaining more knowledge about the nature of your fears can be useful in these situations in order to help allay your worries.

To gain more knowledge in this day and age is quite simple and effective if you really want to find out more information. There are many books out there (like this one!) for you to read and learn from. There are many professionals who can help you; doctors, counsellors, therapists, etc. Also, in this age of technology, the internet is a wonderful tool for gleaning information.

Always remember that 'Knowledge and Information equates to Power'... And for you, this means the Power to Change, for the better:

INFORMATION = POWER = CHANGE

Use of Comparisons

Comparisons can also help you view your thinking from a different perspective. When you worry or are fearful in a particular situation, focus on seeing yourself behave in the way you would be behaving without having the fear. Convince yourself you can function in the way that you want to, without having the negativity and fear that usually accompany your actions. By comparing *yourself* to the perfect/optimal you, you can question your negative assumptions, enabling you to illustrate the sort of thinking errors you are making. After all, if you can see yourself **as you want to be**, the process of eliminating unwanted feelings and emotions becomes easier.

For example, if you are overly defensive or confrontational in certain situations, and you would like to behave differently, then picture yourself as the perfect/optimal you before you encounter a situation and imagine how you would react and speak as the *perfect* you.

Let us say every time you meet up with your mother and it ends up in an argument, you *already* know beforehand what the triggers will be (after all, you've had many years of practice). Imagine yourself hearing something you don't like and NOT reacting to it. Imagine keeping calm and not discussing confrontational subjects. Imagine yourself smiling and saying "It's time to leave", instead of the normal screaming and shouting when you depart. Once you see it, you can be it. Remember, it takes TWO people to argue, so if you really want a situation to change, then start with yourself. You can only change yourself in this world, and not other people.

This technique really involves comparing yourself as you are, to the *perfect/optimal you* that you want to be and can be.

Use of Humor

In my work as a psychotherapist, I sometimes use humor to alleviate any negative or fearful thoughts my clients may have. Using humor together with cognitive-behavioral techniques, I try to get my clients to put their thinking into a more realistic perspective by helping them to see a situation is not as bad or stressful as they have perceived it to be. You too can do the same. To achieve this, try exaggerating your negative internal dialogue to a *ridiculous/sarcastic/funny* level. What I mean here is this:

If you feel you have really done badly in a certain situation, try to humorously envisage the *worst case* scenario for yourself and compare it to what you actually did in that situation… In a humorous way, show yourself it could have been a lot worse! That may make you see the reality of your situation.

Of course, use humor judiciously. Use it to address your unrealistic thinking. It's not a critique of you as a person, but rather a way for you to question your self-deprecating thought processes without any angst or negativity attached to what you're thinking.

Let us say you went on a first date and felt it was a little awkward for you. Instead of beating yourself up about it – "Oh he didn't like me, I shouldn't have worn that dress, I wish I was more intelligent; Why can't I think of funny things to say at the right time?" and feelings to that effect, try to dissimulate your thoughts with humor:

"Well it could have gone a lot worse- he didn't leave after five minutes! I wasn't exactly badly dressed and made no effort ... Even he could see that! It wasn't as if he found me really boring, he DID laugh at some of my funny stories and show interest in me. You know what, it's HIS loss if I don't hear from him ... and he did take my number, so let me see if he's smart enough to call me. Hmm, when I think about it, maybe it wasn't as bad a date as I thought it was ..."

You can see that by using humor in your analysis of a situation, you deflect negative and self-critical thoughts. This results in a fairer assessment of a situation, and one that doesn't reinforce your self-defeating preconceptions.

Role Models (Modelling)

Modelling is a technique used in psychotherapy, whereby a person observes a 'Model' behaving in a certain manner and then attempts to copy/ imitate that behaviour.

How can this benefit you?

Sometimes a good way for you to gauge how accurate your feelings and responses are, is to model your behavior and thinking against how other people may respond or react to a given stimulus. If you are upset or fearful about something, then try to *adopt* the behaviour and thinking of someone whose reactions enable you to consider realistic alternative ways of thinking, to those of your own. It will enable you to see that your feelings and reactions to a given situation are not the only ones possible and that there are other viable, more beneficial ways for you to view the situation. In this instance, the other people that I have mentioned could relate to friends, family members, or even people in the public eye. In reality, it equates to positive behavioral patterns that you can adopt or imitate and which will enhance you in your daily interactions.

Many sociologists and psychologists believe that *Modelling* is the fundamental learning process involved in all societies. We see it in all walks of life and at all different stages of human development. From the little girl who starts to walk in her mother's shoes and starts to copy her mother putting on make-up, to the little boy copying his father every morning shaving in the mirror; Adolescent girls start to mimic the clothes and hairstyles of their favourite singers, whilst adolescent boys start to copy the sporting moves of their favourite sports stars. In the workplace, everyone begins to model themselves on the more successful employees (Mentor – Protégé roles for example), whilst advertisers use famous people to *endorse* their products, so that the buyer feels a sense of pride and togetherness by emulating and imitating the famous person's use of the product.

Role Playing

Another technique that may help you in your negative or fearful thinking is to imagine yourself as a therapist every time you engage in negative thought processes. This method will help you generate and practice realistic answers to negative or fearful thoughts. This will result in you trying to find solutions and answers to your problems when help elsewhere is not available. I have used this technique with clients many times with great success. By doing this, you will teach yourself that whenever fear or negativity enters your mind, it will immediately start the process of self-help, rather than it leading to further negative or debilitating thinking.

As a therapist would do, imagine yourself asking questions, trying to understand your responses and then giving yourself advice. Or imagine you are advising a friend who has the same problem as you have. What would you do? What would you say? What would you advise? Many times, we have the answers to our problems within us, it is just our emotions that cloud our judgments. If we could try to disengage emotionally, then our rationality will function a lot better, and many of the solutions we crave for our problems would be a lot clearer for us. Creating new roles for ourselves could help us find the answers we are looking for.

Imagery Methods of Modifying Your Negative/ Fearful Thinking

You can use imagery at three different stages of your 'mental disputing' process.

1. Imagery can be used to help you with creating alternatives to your negative thinking.

2. Imagery can be used to check the challenges to negative thinking.

3. Imagery can be used to rehearse alternatives to negative thinking.

Creating Alternatives to Negative Thinking

The aim of this technique, is to help you create alternatives to your negative and fearful thinking. It can also be used to show you the connection between your negative thinking and emotional upset.

Imagine yourself in a negative/ fearful situation, and then try to experience the same fears and emotions that you would normally experience in that given situation. Then *change* your extreme negative reactions and feelings to less disturbing and more appropriate feelings.

Examples:

- Change from Anxiety to Concern

- Change from Fear to Apprehension

- Change from Anger to Annoyance

- Change from Depression to Sadness

In fact, you can change any negative emotion you feel to a less extreme version. This change in feeling will usually come about when you change your thinking about the event which created such a strong reaction within you in the first place.

This technique not only helps you create alternatives to your fearful or negative thinking, but it will also help you feel more in control over your emotional upsets. In reality, your thoughts and responses have been conditioned by you. You have automatically reacted a certain way to your thoughts. So it stands to reason that if you change how you think about certain events that elicited your previous responses your automatic reactions and feelings *now* will also change to mirror your new thoughts.

Example:

Every time you think of your ex-spouse you are filled with Anger. You think of the unfair divorce settlement, the hassle and legal expenses of the divorce and the grief that he/she caused you. When you think of this, your blood pressure rises, your heart beats faster and you feel extremely upset.

Instead of Anger, change your thinking to Annoyance.

Now, every time you think of your ex-spouse, you are filled with Annoyance instead. You think of all the time you wasted with him/her, their unreasonable demands on you and their annoying habits. When you think of this, you're glad you no longer have to see your ex, you're relieved this person is out of your life and you feel sorry for the next person who gets involved with him/her! Also, this *relief* leaves you feeling contented, rather than feeling upset.

Can you see that if you change your negative thoughts to a less disturbing and more appropriate feeling, then the resulting outcome will be both physiologically and psychologically more beneficial for you?

(In the above example please note that ex-spouse can more than easily be replaced by an ex-partner!)

Assessing Change

After you challenge your negative and fearful beliefs, you can check to see if you have changed your resultant behaviour and emotions. You can do this by means of an Imagery Exercise.

Let us say that you have a negative belief that produces a generalized emotional upset in you. For example, you are depressed about being fearful in general. In this scenario, it could well be sufficient for you to question whether you feel any better as a result of *disputing* your negative thinking. If however, your upset is very *situationally specific*, for example, you have anxiety about being in public, then you are less likely to feel the upset about the situation when you are, let's say, at home. In this example, it may be helpful for you to imagine yourself back in that fearful situation to check if your feelings associated with that situation have changed.

Imaginal Rehearsal of Alternatives to Fearful/ Negative Thinking

OK, so now that you have learned to dispute a particular thought or belief, you can practice using these alternative thoughts which you have created, by imagining yourself using these new thoughts in a fearful or angst-ridden situation. So, imagine yourself facing the problem situation, and experience the emotional upset associated with this situation. After this, practice the new realistic thinking in your imagination, and observe the changes in your emotional reactions.

This technique can be used to help you become more assured in your realistic thinking, and it's especially useful if you cannot *see* yourself facing up to your fears successfully. Another benefit of this *Imaginal Technique* is that, when you successfully confront your fears, it will also increase your belief that you are able to control situations and emotions to your advantage, thus increasing your levels of confidence when faced with the situation that previously concerned you.

Distraction

Another useful tool for your repertoire of *Facing Your Fears* is Distraction. It's the skill of blocking out fears and self-defeating thinking, by simply thinking of something else.

You may not be in a situation whereby you can constantly challenge your negative thinking. Let's say, for example, you are self-conscious about what other people think of you, and you find yourself in a situation where you are talking to someone. A good coping strategy here would be to distract yourself from your self-conscious thoughts, by *concentrating* on what the other person is saying. Of course in some situations it's quicker for you to use distraction techniques rather than disputing techniques, but it would be a good idea for you to make a mental note of these situations so that later on, you can dispute any negative thinking.

A good time for you to use this distraction technique is when you may be experiencing extreme emotional turmoil. For example, if you are in a panic over something, you may not be able to start disputing your negative thoughts. However, to alleviate your distress, what you can do is become mindful of your thoughts, and then actively distract yourself from that train of thought. *Immediately start to think of something else to take your thoughts away from what is upsetting you.* Once you have calmed down, then you can challenge and dispute your negative thoughts and beliefs.

Note: For future occurrences of the problematic situation, you can use your realistic alternative thoughts that you have created through your disputing and challenging... And you can rehearse these alternative thoughts before you next find yourself in the problematic situation.

Behavioral Methods of Modifying Your Negative/ Fearful Thinking

Perhaps the best way for you to modify negative thinking is to *behave* in a way that counteracts your negative thinking. You can test your responses to situations that you have found fearful by carrying out behavioral tasks and evaluating the outcome. Here are a few examples:

- The person who is afraid of commitment puts himself into situations where commitment is required.

- The person who is fearful of being in public puts herself into a position to venture out into a social/public environment.

- The person who is a perfectionist and is afraid to make mistakes, allows himself to make deliberate mistakes.

- The person who may be afraid of being rejected, allows herself to be exposed to situations where she may be rejected.

If we look at the last example, being in situations where you might be rejected will provide you with the opportunity to learn:

a) That you can withstand rejection

b) That rejection does not diminish you as a person

c) That rejection isn't as bad as you imagine/envisage it to be

You can carry out such behavioral tasks for yourself, and over time evaluate your responses to stimuli such as anxiety, stress, fear, etc., with the result being that you will eventually overcome your fears and worries, by being better able to monitor them.

Modifying Activating Events for Your Emotional Problems

In Cognitive-Behavioral Therapy, there is a basic model that is used by all therapists in their work. It is called the **ABC** model. You too can learn this to help you combat fears, negative thinking and any other maladaptive behaviour pattern. It was first put forward by Ellis (1977) and explains the relationship between thinking and emotions. Here is an overview of how it works:

Activating Event (**A**) leads to emotional and behavioral Consequences (**C**) – with the emotional consequences being mediated by your Beliefs (**B**).

Here's an example:

Imagine you are out shopping and a friend walks by without acknowledging you. As a result, you feel depressed.

The **ABC** analysis is as follows:

A = Activating Event: Friend fails to acknowledge you

B = Belief:

(a) inferences- "My friend has ignored me."
"She must be angry with me."
"She probably now dislikes me."

(b) evaluation- "It's terrible if a friend dislikes you and you lose a friendship"

C = Consequence (emotional): Depression

Consequence (behavioral): Future avoidance of Friend

Let us analyze this scenario in a little more depth. Of course in the above situation, there could be many plausible explanations as to why your friend has ignored you, other than those inferences drawn on by you. Maybe your friend didn't see you as she was deep in thought; maybe she had just had an argument with her partner and ignores everyone when she is upset like this. Let's say your friend deliberately did ignore you, your conclusion that she doesn't like you may not be true. Also, your evaluation that it is terrible if someone doesn't like you may be exaggerated.

In these types of examples, it's important for you to not create self-fulfilling prophecies by jumping to conclusions. If you *think* your friend doesn't like you, you may become distant towards her. Your friend may pick up on your aloofness, interpret it as you being unfriendly, and then reciprocate the same distance towards you. As a result, you may see this as confirmation and evidence of your original conclusion. So, by jumping to conclusions, you have created a self-fulfilling prophecy, with the outcome being that what you didn't want to happen, has happened!

Result = You may have lost a friend because you didn't take the necessary steps to find out what your friend's preoccupations were at that time.

So far when it comes to *facing your fears* we have looked mostly at your Beliefs in dealing with problems you may have. Looking more closely at the **ABC** model, we will focus a little more on changing your Activating events when it comes to helping you deal with what is holding you back in your life.

Maybe you create your own 'Activating Events' for yourself by lacking skills in solving your personal problems, or you may have poor social skills. It could be your situation awareness is also poor, so you find it difficult to work out your environment. Let's look at a few more case studies briefly and work out what is truly going on.

* Melissa is a true 'people-pleaser'. She finds it very difficult to say 'no' to people and always tries her best to make everyone happy, so that in return she is liked. The problem for her here is that she often gets taken for granted and is used by other people. Her inability to say 'no' is due to her poor social skills, and as a result of this, she often feels bitter, resentful and depressed.

What would you advise Melissa in the above example?

Well done if you said it would be advisable for her to be more assertive and refuse requests, which in turn would lead her to prevent the events that trigger bitterness, resentment and depression in her life.

* George is a married man with many marital problems. He deals with this by drinking heavily, and as a result loses his job because of his alcohol problems. No work or money result in him struggling to cope and this in turn leads to him fighting

every day with his wife. She ends up leaving him and taking the children.

Would you have any sympathy or advice for George?

Well, you could help him by pointing out he needs to tackle his problems more effectively, which in turn would help reduce his behavioral and emotional disturbances by cutting down on the problematic situations which trigger his upsets. This in turn will also lead to less alcohol dependence.

* Jim is depressed because he is lonely. He is single and doesn't have any friends. He has always shied away from people and preferred his own company, but deep down he knows he has missed out immensely on a social life with friends.

How would you analyze Jim?

The Activating Event for his depression is being lonely. However for people in this predicament, it tends to be like a two-edged sword. Being alone could also be a behavioral consequence of his Beliefs, in that he will probably be rejected by people if he tries to make friends (therefore he makes no effort).

It will help you in working through your own fears and negative thinking by being more sympathetic and empathetic towards other people. In overcoming your own maladaptive thinking, understand that it could sometimes be a result of a lack of certain skills on your part, rather than it being all psychologically based. Bear in mind that for you, poor social performances or poor personal problem solving skills are often a combination of skills deficits AND self-defeating thinking. In facing your fears and *overcoming* them, learn not only to modify your beliefs, but also put some emphasis on acquiring new social skills.

Learning New Social Skills

Social skills learning can be defined as:

Acquiring new procedures that can help you communicate more effectively; especially concerned with verbal and non-verbal aspects of conversation and with friendship formation. (Trower et al. 1978).

So what type of new social skills would you need to acquire?

* Being able to keep a conversation going

* Developing your listening skills

* Learning to read social cues

* Being able to use and incorporate social-media skills

* Understanding cultural and social differences

* Being able to interpret and use 'body language'

The best way to improve or learn a new social skill is by focusing on one new skill at a time. While learning this new skill, the best thing to do is to practice using the new skill as much as possible. Always be focused and mindful of what you are actually practicing, until you feel comfortable using it. So for example, if you're focusing on listening, make sure you use all opportunities available to listen to people, and resist the urge to interrupt or speak until the other person has finished. By training yourself to listen, you will eventually become a better listener. In fact training yourself involves the following steps:

1) Identifying the skill that needs to be worked on

2) Understanding the function of the skill, and how or when to use it

3) Imagining yourself with the skill

4) Practicing the use of the skill by yourself (where possible)

5) Trying to gain any feedback (if possible)

6) Using the skill in real-life situations

One area I touched on earlier in the example with Melissa is being more assertive. Learning assertiveness is a social-skill where the emphasis is on you being able to express your feelings, ideas and opinions in a direct but socially acceptable way. You are self-assured and confident in yourself and how you come across, but without being aggressive. Being assertive equates to being able to express your likes and dislikes clearly and directly, in a constructive non-demanding and non-threatening way. The key to being assertive is knowing how to get what you want without disrespecting other people.

Assertiveness training could include the following:

* Learning how to make requests

* Learning how to refuse requests without feeling guilty

* Learning how to deal with criticism

* Learning how to turn people down

* Learning how to express your anger

* Learning how to respect other people's boundaries as well as your own

* Learning how to express and respect appreciation

Here are a couple of Assertiveness Techniques to help you:

1) Use the word "I" in discussions. It's non-confrontational to talk about yourself in a discussion rather than talking about the other person. Talking about other people can be perceived as a 'personal attack'. For example, your best friend ALWAYS arrives late for appointments and meetings. Try speaking like this:

"I get quite upset every time you're late because I make a great effort to be on time and I feel a little disrespected when you're constantly late."

Instead of this:

"You're always late for appointments. You're such a bad time keeper and actually I sometimes wonder if you're late on purpose!"

The first example explains your feelings and paves the way for a positive discussion. The second example can be seen as a personal attack, which can result in a conflictual situation.

2) The 'Scratched Record' technique. In the good old days of vinyl records, a scratch on the record resulted in the same part of the song being played again and again. This technique involves you repeating yourself several times no matter how the other person tries to divert you. It is a good technique for getting what you ordered, bought or asked for. An example could be:

You: "Hello. I am here to check into my room please."
Receptionist: "Yes sir. I see you have room 254."

You: "Thank you. Sounds good. I booked a room with a sea-view. Does it have a sea-view?"

Receptionist: "I'm afraid not sir, but it's a nice room anyway."

You: "I'm sure it is, but I would like a sea-view from my room please."

Receptionist: "254 is a nice room. We've never had any complaints."

You: "I'm sure you haven't, but I would still like a sea-view please."

Receptionist: "OK sir. I will just check the rooms again and find one with a sea-view for you."

You can see in the above example that by persisting, in a non-confrontational manner, you can get what you want. You may point out, what if there were no rooms with a sea-view, then what? Of course in the same manner, you could ask to speak to the manager, ask for a refund, or ask how the hotel can appease you if they have made a genuine mistake. The important part is learning how to get your point across in a non-aggressive way and try to go for a "win-win" scenario where everyone ends up satisfied. In fact, that is the outcome you should strive for in *all* your dealings.

How to Solve Personal Problems

If you are poor at solving problems, especially personal ones, you can learn a series of steps to help you think through problems together with solutions, enabling you to cope with problems in a more constructive way. Although the steps may seem simplistic, I find that with my clients, these steps really do work:

a) Firstly- Define your Problem

b) Secondly- Work out possible solutions to your problem

c) Thirdly- Evaluate the solutions and select the best solution

d) Finally- Plan how to implement your preferred solution.

What I ask my clients to do, is to write down these points on a sheet of paper, leaving spaces under each point, and then either together, or in the client's own time, each step is worked through until a preferred solution is found for whatever problem is presented. The key is to write down all possible solutions, however ridiculous they may seem, and then to work through and evaluate the consequences of the various solutions, until ultimately, the best solution is found. Of course, you can do exactly the same in your own time and with whatever problem you have.

Let's look at an example:

i) Problem: "My relationship is not working out
                            how I had hoped it would".

ii) Possible Solutions: - End the relationship
                            - Separate for a period
                            - Go to Couples Counselling
                            - Ignore the problem
                            - Discuss the situation with my
                              partner

iii) Evaluate Solutions:

- End the relationship – "I don't really want to as I love my husband. If we can work through our problems, I would like us to remain together."

- Separate for a period – "This might give us the space we need, but ultimately it could open the door for us to get used to being away from each other."

- Go to Couples Counselling – "I hate discussing our problems with other people. What can a stranger tell us that we don't already know? On the flip side, maybe some objective advice could really benefit us by showing us something new."

- Ignore the problem – "If I ignore the problem I doubt it would go away. In fact, it would probably get worse and result in us splitting up anyway."

- Discuss the situation with my partner – "I have tried many times talking to him. He refuses to open up to me and it leads to more arguments anyway, so I doubt that would work."

"Going over my options, I think the best solution for me and for us is to try Couples Counselling. That is the only solution that I can see working for us."

iv) Implementing the Solution: "I will talk it over with my husband and then first thing tomorrow morning, I will look for counsellors and set up an appointment. I already feel better now for being pro-active ..."

Working through your problems should be similar to the above example. Please bear in mind though, that you may not find a satisfactory solution to your problem, even though your chosen option may be the best one available for you. These steps will also help you clarify issues at the very least, and help you to set up a mode of tackling problems which you may currently lack.

A final point to note is that, even if your preferred solution doesn't work out the way you envisage, at least you will have a blueprint of possible solutions, and a new skill set for dealing with all your problems and fears, both presently and for the future.

Creating Emotional and Behavioral Changes

The whole point of *Facing Your Fears* and dealing with negative and maladaptive behaviour, is to create changes in your thinking for the better. Just be wary that change doesn't happen overnight. In some cases, you are trying to change a life-time of thinking and behaving in a certain way. Also, if you encounter a problem, your first reaction may be to revert back to 'default'. In order to sustain lasting changes in your emotional life and your behaviour, you must consolidate your realistic beliefs and move from your natural default setting, to be convinced by more optimal functioning beliefs. In other words, you need to 'reboot your mental computer' and change your 'default settings' to ones that enable you to function in a better way; better than you are currently doing so.

The Keys to Emotional and Behavioral Changes are:

* Have conviction in alternative thinking

* Understand the difference between negative beliefs and functional beliefs

* Develop better emotional insight so you understand your feelings more

* Change your core beliefs if need be

* Redefine your thoughts to create different emotional outcomes

"You gain strength, courage and confidence by every experience in which you really stop to look fear in the face. You must do the thing which you think you cannot do."

Eleanor Roosevelt

Now that we have looked at some definitions, techniques and solutions to help you with any of your maladaptive, negative and fearful thoughts, we will look at a few more case studies. This time, when you read them, try to work out the underlying issues each person has and what you would recommend for them to help them overcome their issues. Remember, the better you are at working out problems and finding solutions in other people's lives, the easier it will be for you to implement the necessary steps in finding the best solutions for you in your life.

Case studies:

* Mario is forty-two years old. He works in The City of London for a European bank and he often travels a lot on business trips. He is married with a child and lives in a North London together with his wife and a live-in au pair. Again, looking at Mario's life from the outside, it is difficult to see what his worries and fears may be.

"I am from the south of Europe, so for me, it was difficult to leave my family and relocate to London. I am very close to my mother in particular, and I think my wife is threatened by this. She doesn't like me talking on the phone to my mother and always creates problems. In fact my family don't like my wife and she doesn't like them in return. I am stuck in the middle really. Although I love my wife, I can't see a way out. Actually I have already prepared for the day we may split. I don't want to live alone and be apart from my child, but maybe that is for the best. I worry about how my home life affects my child. I am also fearful of divorce. My wife will definitely go after my money for sure. In fact, to be honest, I don't trust my wife on any level. Maybe she is cheating on me also. I just don't know what to think anymore. I am consumed with worry and I am fearful every single day."

Mario's daily existence is racked with fear and worry. Can you relate to any of his concerns? How would you analyze his situation and what advice would you give to him?

* Penelope is sixty-two years old. A couple of years previously she suffered a major illness which left her totally debilitated. In fact she was very close to losing her life. As a result, she has stopped working and is now focused on living her life to its fullest. She travels a lot, is engaged in her sons' lives, and she is looking to be more altruistic. Maybe Penelope's fears might seem obvious to you, or maybe her worries are not what you would expect…

"I have lived a wonderful life and enjoyed some fantastic experiences. I have been with some wonderful men and enjoyed their company. My work life has been very interesting and I have had some wonderful clients in my time. I feel I have been given a second chance at life and now want to put into place all the things that will facilitate my life and that of my sons. The main problem though is that there is a big void in my life. I really don't know what to do with my free time. I am at a loss and without direction. For the first time in my life I feel empty and depressed about what I have gone through physically and emotionally. I put on a brave face for everyone, but deep down I grieve at the losses I have suffered physically. I am not able to do what I did before. In my darker moments, I think 'Why me?'… Life just isn't fair. Maybe I have another ten years left according to my doctors. I am sad for my sons but don't show them how scared I am for the future. I wish I wasn't so fearful about what the future has in store for me."

Unfortunately for Penelope, her future seems limited compared to how her life was before she suffered her illness. Sometimes our lives can take a dramatic turn which leaves us questioning everything about our existence and it can also create stresses we never imagined possible.

If you are going through similar life dilemmas to Penelope, then hopefully you now have some beneficial tools that will help you find the resolutions you are looking for. Let us now take a look at Lauren's life:

* Lauren is fifty years old. She lives with her two sons in the suburbs. Although she is not married, she lived with her common law partner until he left her recently for another woman. She works part-time and has a very large extended family that help her with the upbringing of her sons. Her concerns about her life are quite interesting. Can you relate to Lauren's predicament?

"My partner works in the music industry and is away a lot. I know he cheated on me on many occasions, but I accepted it. I mean, you can't expect a man to be away on tour and not get up to anything. I forgave his indiscretions. After all he was a good provider for the boys and we had a good lifestyle. However, after all our time together he left me for a woman that he worked with. I am so angry. Not with him, but with her! She *knew* he was involved with someone else. She has deprived my boys of being with their father. The worst thing is, is that I can't compete with her. How do you compete with a woman who has everything? I am not happy at the situation and I will make him suffer. I have stopped him seeing the boys, and if she comes anywhere near me, I don't know what I will do. I don't know how this will work out, but I am really angry for my boys' sakes, and I don't know how I will take care of them and provide for them. Surely boys need their fathers don't they? How will I cope with raising them by myself?"

Lauren is trapped in the consequences of her partner's actions. Her fears don't just relate to her but also for the upbringing of her sons. What are her options? Are you or anyone you know in a similar situation to her? How would you overcome the difficulties that she now faces?

Now that we have looked at ways for you to move forwards from the many fears that have hindered you from achieving what you want to in your life, it's important you always remain *mindful* of the following fact: The strength in overcoming your problems *already* lies within you...

"Believe in Yourself!

Have faith in your abilities!

Without a humble but reasonable confidence in your own powers, you cannot be successful or happy."

Norman Vincent Peale

CHAPTER TWO:

GOING FOR YOUR GOALS

"A goal is a desired result a person or a system envisions, plans and commits to achieve, a personal or organisational desired end-point in some sort of assumed development. Many people endeavor to reach goals within a finite time by setting deadlines.

It is roughly similar to a purpose or aim, the anticipated result which guides reaction, or an end ... that has intrinsic value."

Wikipedia

* Orla is forty-nine years old and has drifted throughout her life. She has never been materialistic and never dreamed of settling down. She has had a few broken relationships and never saw herself as having children. Being from a traditional family, she is the youngest of three sisters and she has always been the joker of the family.

"I guess I always knew things would work out for me one way or another, so I never had to make any real, true commitments. I have never wanted children and never planned to have them. It is too late for me now anyway, so that's not an option anymore. My living situation has always been tough. I live with three other girls. I rent. I have never wanted my own place. I want to find a rich man. Someone to take care of me. My family live in Ireland but I don't want to go back. My other sisters are very settled with husbands, children and houses. Good luck to them. I'm not jealous, but if I'm honest, I do envy them a little. I think the problem in my life has been that I have just "gone with the flow". I have procrastinated all my life and have never really had any goals. I have recently lost my job as my place of work has closed down. I don't really know what I want to do with myself. I have drifted for too long and it has all caught up with me as I'm not getting any younger ..."

In Orla's case, because she has never really had any goals in her life, she finds herself in a not too good a position as she approaches the age of fifty. She shares rented accommodation, doesn't have children, is looking for a new place of employment, and has no aims or direction. Her only real goal is to meet a man with money.

Many people find themselves in a similar position to Orla. They have drifted through life, not taking it seriously and find themselves full of regrets. They will eventually end up in loveless relationships because their partners have money, or they will end up doing things they don't want to because their opportunities become more and more limited.

However, it's never too late to redefine yourself or your life. Even in the above example, it's not too late for Orla to turn her life around. Apart from wanting a 'rich man' to save her, she could easily create a new set of parameters to help her out of her predicament.

* Simon is forty-five years old. He has been caught up with family dramas all of his life. He has been involved in dealing with his parents' relationship and their problems, together with trying to maintain a good relationship with his brothers. Unfortunately, his sister passed away a few years previously, which had a major impact on him and his family. His personal life has been pretty convoluted over the years also. He is now involved in a long distance relationship.

"I have always seen myself as a pioneer and a maverick. I haven't wanted to do what 'normal' people do. My life has been full of opportunities but I don't think I have taken any of them as I should have. Maybe I have had too many choices and too many things going on in my life which have resulted in me not being able to focus on one thing. Maybe I have been a jack of all trades and have not been able to focus on relationships, friendships or even work. The death of my sister knocked me and my family back. For a long time there was a lot of anger, blame and guilt. That stopped me making decisions I should have. My goals were put on hold and I don't really have any tangible aims anymore. To make matters worse, I will be a father for the first time in a few months, but I am enmeshed in helping out my family in England. As my partner lives abroad, she needs my help and support. I am continually travelling backwards and forwards and that will be my life for the foreseeable future. I used to have so many goals in my life, but now, I don't know what I should be doing, or which direction I should be heading in."

For Simon, circumstances such as parental problems, bereavement, a long distance relationship and impending fatherhood have meant that for many years, his decision making has been clouded and his goals for the future have been put on hold. Any plans he may have had, have become victim to the circumstances he now finds himself in, and rather than being proactive in his decision-making and goal-setting, he has become reactive to what 'fate' has thrown at him.

Sometimes in life, maybe our futures become difficult for us to see, and we may need guidance to show us the possibilities.

Setting ourselves goals can be a way of us gauging if we are heading in the right direction. After all, at some point in our lives, we all may have dreamt of:

- Starting our own businesses

- Meeting the right person for us

- Travelling the world

- Being successful

- Winning the lottery

But the difference between dreams and goals is that goals need action, focus and deadlines which can produce results. Dreams are just imaginary thoughts with no end product and no finish lines. They are in effect, just *Dreams* ...

Goals require hard-work and in reality can lead to life-changing outcomes.

Of course, many goals can start out as dreams, but from dreams to reality, something needs to be done, a plan of action needs to be created, otherwise our dreams remain as something within our thoughts, which never see the light of day. Put it this way, every person living 'the life they dreamed of', started out with an idea, sometimes it remained a pipe dream for a long time, but then, *they did something about it!* And what they did was to turn those dreams into goals and then into reality.

"It isn't sufficient just to want. You've got to ask yourself what you are going to do to get the things you want."

Richard D. Rosen

The key to understanding and implementing a goal, is to make it achievable and to make it SMART! A SMART goal can be defined as follows:

Specific

Measurable

Attainable

Realistic

Timely

Specific:

A specific goal will help you achieve what you want to, rather than some sort of general goal or desire which can be unattainable. Setting specific goals is important, and to accomplish this, you need to answer the following six "W" questions.

When: Create a time frame.

Where: Identify a location.

Which: Identify your requirements and limitations.

Who: Who is involved?

What: What do I want to accomplish?

Why: Work out specific reasons and benefits for accomplishing your goals.

Examples:

A General Goal for you would be: "I need to lose weight".

A Specific Goal would state, "I will join a slimming group and aim to lose at least 2lbs a week."

General Goal: "One day I will read that best-selling book that I've been meaning to …"

Specific Goal: "Tomorrow after work, I will begin reading my book and then start reading a minimum of ten pages a day until I have finished it …"

Measurable:

It's important you create concrete criteria for measuring your progress towards attaining each goal that you set yourself.

Measuring your progress means that you stay on track and once you reach your target dates, the happiness and excitement this creates in you will spur you on with the continued effort that you need to accomplish your goals.

You need some parameters to determine if your goal is measurable, and to do this, you must ask yourself questions, such as:

How many?

How much?

How often?

How will I know when my goal is accomplished?

Examples: You may need to ask yourself, "How many hours a day do I need to revise before I take my exam? ... I need at least two hours a day."

Or

"How much time per week can I devote to learning a language? ... I can devote between three to five hours per week."

Once you have worked out the viable parameters and criteria for yourself, then you have to make sure you stick to them!

Attainable:

As stated earlier, most goals tend to start out as just dreams. Once you figure out which goals are most important to you, you can figure out ways to make them become reality. To make this happen, you need to develop:

*Your Attitude-

This entails thinking yourself into being the person who is successful.

*Your Skills-

Improve and develop the skills necessary for you in being able to attain your goals.

*Your Abilities-

Improve and develop your talents to give you the power to achieve your goals.

*Your Financial Situation (in order to help you reach your goals)-

Make sure your finances can support you over the time frame required to accomplish your goals.

You must be able to see all opportunities available to you (some may have been previously overlooked by you) in order for you to achieve your goals.

In your life, you can reach goals you set yourself when you plan each step wisely and allow yourself a time frame to carry out your steps. As you grow in confidence, goals that may have seemed unattainable and out of reach, suddenly begin to appear attainable. It's important to list your goals or visualize them, so that it builds your self-image. After all, this will allow you to see yourself as worthy of your goals, and therefore will help you develop the personality and traits that you need in moving towards attaining them.

Realistic:

To be realistic, a goal must represent an objective to which you are:

- Able to work for

- Willing to work for

Your goals can be both high and realistic. Remember, YOU are the only one who can determine just how high and just how realistic your goals should be. You also need to be sure that every goal you have represents substantial progress for you as you head in the right direction.

Paradoxically, a high goal is often easier to reach than a low goal. Why? Well, because unsurprisingly, a low goal exerts a lower motivational force in you. The more you push yourself, the more you tend to achieve. Your goals are like your personal boundaries- the more you exert yourself, the more you will accomplish. Think back over your life and you'll notice that your greatest achievements have come from the hardest adversities you have faced. Once you have the force to achieve what you want, something that seemed difficult from the offset works out easier to do than you ever imagined it would be.

Example: You have always dreamed of baking for a living as you have been very good at it throughout your life. You want to start your own business baking cakes and supplying them to local businesses in your area. You know that with this goal, you are *now* at the stage of your life where you are *able* and *willing* to work for it to make it a reality, which it can ultimately become.

Timely:

It's important for you that you fix your goal into a defined time frame. With no time frame attached, you don't know where you are in terms of achieving it. Going back to the earlier example of losing weight, let us say you want to lose 20lbs. What is your time frame? "Some point soon ..." That won't work. You need specifics. Set yourself a date. "I need to lose 20lbs by the 1st of June." Or as I mentioned earlier, if you want to lose 20lbs and you aim to lose 2lbs a week, then give yourself ten weeks from when you start, and continue losing the desired weight every week. Once you have your timeframe anchored, your subconscious mind starts to work on achieving your goal.

Ultimately your goal is deemed realistic if you ***truly believe*** that you can reach it. Another good way for you to understand your capabilities is to see if you have done anything similar in the past, or ask yourself what conditions need to exist for you to attain your goals.

Example: If you have already achieved something similar in the past, you have created the neurological pathways in your mind that lead you to repeating the same goals again, or even surpassing them. Having a deep rooted confidence results in you being able to truly believe you can repeat prior successes. Sports men and women, for example, work on this premise. Once they have achieved a personal best, they repeat the same training, but with renewed confidence and belief, because they now know that they can eventually surpass their previous best achievements.

Otherwise, it's important for you to work out the conditions you need to reach your goals. With perseverance, confidence and an understanding of your surroundings, you will be able to truly believe your goals can become reality.

T can also represent **Tangible** – Your goals are deemed tangible when you can experience them with any one of your senses:

- Sight

- Smell

- Touch

- Taste

- Hearing

Tangible goals have a better chance of being specific for you, as well as measurable. Ultimately this means they are more attainable and realistic for you to accomplish. When you think about it logically, it's only natural that tangible paradigms are easier to keep track of rather than thought based ones.

It's important when you are chasing your goals to remain positive and focused as your way of thinking is paramount.

"The quality of your thinking determines the quality of your life."

A. R. Bernard

The Importance of Mindset

The word *mindset* is bandied about a lot in general conversation. Either in positive or negative contexts, it's used to explain how someone's form or performance has been affected by their way of thinking.

"She did really well at the interview today. She seemed sharp and focused. Her *mindset* appeared to be perfect."

"Unfortunately for him, he failed in his efforts. His *mindset* didn't seem quite right today."

Of course, when it comes to going for and achieving your goals, your mindset is clearly a determining factor in whether you attain them or not. If we look at the concept of your mindset in greater depth, we can break it down to the methods, notations or assumptions that you hold. When you establish the right mindset in going after your goals, this creates a powerful incentive for you that enables you to adopt prior behaviors, choices and tools, which then propel you towards the accomplishment of what you're striving for.

People who have reached their goals or who are seen as high achievers tend to have a way of thinking, a *mindset* that includes having the ability to form a strong consensus, which is coupled with powerful negotiating skills. They are also very good at following and adopting the mindset of other high achievers. This can come under the guise of *Modelling* which we looked at previously. It makes sense that if you want to achieve your goals, a sure fire way of doing this is to adopt the traits of someone who has done it previously. After all, the wheel was invented only ONCE! Everything else that has followed has been a variation and improvement on the original design. The same rule applies to achieving your goals. Whatever it is that you want to accomplish, be it losing weight, getting married, starting your business, looking for a new job, getting your invention patented, sharing your visions with the world, studying, becoming an actor, changing your career, etc., etc., someone else before you has had the same goal at some point and achieved it! Surely it makes sense to adopt the mindset of such an achiever as you pursue your goals...

After all, it doesn't seem quite so strange in trying to attain your goals when you can focus on or see other people who are doing it or have done it before you. Adopt the following mentality and mindset in your endeavors:

"If he/she can do it, why can't I?!"

Adopt this stubborn way of thinking, don't back down and don't give up! Make this your Philosophy of Life. Always remember ...

"If he/she can do it, why can't I?!"

Idea Flows

When you are full of energy and your inner motivation levels to do something are extremely high, this will then give you the power to zone into your thoughts and help you create what I call *Idea Flows*.

Idea flows are a constant flow of ideas and possibilities that appear to you and are powered by your motivation to achieve. You then become so engrossed at the energy your ideas create, that you become compelled to see them through. Your desire and motivational levels become extremely high, enabling you to break through with your ideas. This desire and motivation allows you long periods of concentration and hard work in pushing towards your goals. Another way to look at it, is by calling it *Dynamism*. You become dynamic as you chase your ideas and goals until they become reality.

Dynamism > Ideas > Goals > Reality

Another by-product of chasing success and goals is that it makes you more of a risk taker. For example:

If your goal is to work for yourself or start your own business, you are more likely to take certain risks to accomplish those goals. These could involve financial risks, relationship risks, career risks, etc. Also, because you become more driven to accomplish what you have started, it doesn't matter to you if the risk required seems ambiguous or uncertain, you will follow through with it and see it through anyway.

"It had long since come to my attention, that people of accomplishment rarely sat back and let things happen to them. They went out and happened to things."

Leonardo da Vinci

It's important to put your Mindset and ideas into the right context for achieving your goals. The following table sums it up perfectly:

Chances of Success

0% = I won't

10% = I can't

20% = I don't know how

30% = I wish I could

40% = I want to

50% = I think I might

60% = I might

70% = I think I can

80% = I can

90% = I am

100% = I DID

Although the above table may seem simplistic, it really does sum up perfectly your chances of success according to how you yourself view the possible outcome. You only ever achieve your goals in life, once you've seen them through. There are of course certain mental blocks you may have when it comes to turning your dreams into attainable goals and into reality. What are they and how should you deal with them?

Mental Blocks

1. "I fear I'm not good enough."

We looked in greater detail at dealing with your fears in Chapter One. What is important to know here is that you shouldn't confuse natural questioning and 'performance anxiety' with genuine *fear*. Whatever you keep striving for, whatever you stretch your capabilities with, whatever new risks you take in life, you may experience some temporary emotional change, but this is all part of the process of *Growth*.

2. "How do I get rid of the anxiety of doing something?"

Although this sounds like a complex mental block, the solution is pretty simple. The only way to rid yourself of this type of anxiety, is just to go out and DO whatever you have dreamed of doing! You need to confront the worry of doing something specific with *action* before any emotions like anxiety start to dissipate. Once you begin the process of *doing*, your natural sense of accomplishment will push away any doubts and anxieties you may have.

3. "Will I feel better about myself if I pursue my dreams and goals?"

As in the previous mental block, the answer to this doubt is also pretty straightforward. If you start to focus on attaining what you truly desire, you WILL feel better about yourself. Once the wheels of action are in motion, not only do your doubts, worries and anxieties go away, but your self-image and levels of self-confidence receive a massive boost. You will feel as if your life has a new meaning and purpose.

4. "This is all pretty unfamiliar territory for me!"

Don't worry too much about being out of your comfort zone. Just understand that EVERYONE who has pursued their goals has at some point been in pretty unfamiliar territory. Many people who seem calm and confident have either worried or still worry every time they pursue their goals. Just remember all *masters* started out as *apprentices* at some point. Everyone who has achieved something in their lives felt apprehension, but did what they had to do anyway. To overcome the fear of the unfamiliar, retrain your thoughts by constantly repeating to yourself, "Just because I haven't done it before, doesn't mean I can't do it now." Keep saying this to yourself until it becomes a part of your way of thinking.

5. "Is pushing through my fears of risk worse than any regrets I may have for not pursuing my goals?"

What do you think is a worse feeling? The fear of pursuing your goals? Or the regret of not going after them? So the main fear in pursuing your goals is what exactly? Failure? If you fail, then at least you can say you tried. In fact, failure may be the precursor to success anyway. If you've failed, you can use the experience to tweak, adapt or change certain aspects of your failure and turn it into success. In life, if you get knocked down nine times, then get up ten times. Remember, success isn't guaranteed, but failure isn't permanent or fatal either. Whatever setbacks you face in life, say to yourself, "I can handle them, I can get over them". Don't let any fears hinder you from pursuing your goals and ultimately stop you from changing your life into the one that you have always envisaged. Every great inventor, every great entrepreneur and every great achiever has been knocked back MANY times before success finally came knocking on their door. Also, over the years I have met and worked with many people who have regretted not pursuing their dreams and goals. Don't be one of them! Eventually, time catches up with us all, and the last thing you ever want is the feeling of helplessness and hopelessness which regret will invariably bring you.

"The strongest people aren't always the people who win, but the people who don't give up when they lose."

Liam Payne

CHAPTER THREE:

EMPOWERMENT

Empowerment is a word that has been used many times over the years covering a vast array of subjects from motivational sciences, philosophy, sociology, psychology, feminism and self-help. We will look at various definitions and how they may help you in your life.

The idea of empowerment refers to giving you power or authority in official, legal or psychological areas. The general meaning behind it is that it gives you assertion and enablement in various situations. The process involves moving from a point of inactivity or inertia, to a revitalized and energetic position where you feel capable of achievement …

"We cannot become what we need to be, by remaining what we are."

Max De Pree

* Mo is forty-nine years old. He comes from a traditional Asian family, with strong values and roles. Growing up he was always quiet, observant and obedient. He never rebelled or caused his family any problems. He wasn't naturally studious, but always tried his best and eventually passed his exams after failing a couple of times. In his work life, he has always respected authority and has been respectful of his bosses. He has never questioned his managers and has accepted their decisions and orders. He remains unmarried as he struggles to connect with women and his shyness has contributed to the awkwardness he feels when interacting with the opposite sex.

"I have never really spoken up for myself in my life. I guess in many ways people have walked all over me. I have let people get away with certain behaviors that I have found unacceptable, but I have never said or done anything about it. At work, I have always done what my bosses have asked of me. I mean, you never question your bosses, do you?

I have never had a proper relationship with a woman. I am waiting to find the right woman for me so I can settle down into married life. I have been on a few dates and things like that, but I never seem to be successful with women. I sometimes wonder if my life will remain as it is. I am not too fulfilled at work, I rent a room in a house owned by my landlord, and I can't seem to find someone to share my life with. Deep down I would like a wife who is similar to my mother. I am very close to her and would like another relationship where I feel loved and needed. I sometimes wish I had the power and energy to turn my life around ... I feel so helpless sometimes."

There are many people like Mo, who feel trapped in an unfulfilled life, with few friends and no significant partner to share their life with. They lack the impetus or energy that they require to turn things around for the better in their lives. Their days become repetitive with an underlying sense of hopelessness, as they know that unless they do something to change their day-to-day existence, their lives will continue to be just as unfulfilling as the previous day, week, month and year.

* Kat is fifty-five years old. She is from a Mediterranean country in the south of Europe originally. She moved to England to get married when she was nineteen, but unfortunately for her, her husband turned out to be both

unreliable and disrespectful towards her. She ended up having five children with him, but he was always physically and emotionally abusive to her. Despite his behaviour, she remained in the marriage, even though he cheated on her many times and eventually left her for another woman. Her children have urged her to be more proactive and seek a divorce and try to move on in her life, but she remains married to him, unwilling and unable to find the motivation and force needed to take the next step in her life.

"All I ever wanted to do was to get married and have children. I never had any ambitions in my life. Where I come from, women tend to just want to be housewives. It's changing now, but I haven't really changed. I don't want a divorce, because I feel if you get married it should be for life irrespective of what happens. My children, especially my daughters, have tried to help me, but I guess deep down, I don't really want to be helped. I don't really know why I have put up with my husband's cheating and abuse. When you go to another country, I guess it is difficult to be a part of that country. You have to learn a new language, a new culture and a new way of being. For me, I have always been laid back and accepted things. The women in this country seem to know their rights and what they are entitled to, but I have never been pushy like that. People talk of women's rights and empowerment, but I don't really understand any of that. Maybe I do need to be empowered, but what does that mean and entail... also, how does somebody like me go about doing that?"

For Kat, although it has been a hard life, she has managed to cope. Ironically, although she seems weak, she has had to be very strong to deal with the difficulties in her life. If she developed new skills and became *empowered*, surely for her, life would be far more rewarding.

Maybe in your life, in certain areas, you may be able to relate to Mo or Kat. For you, it may just be a question of developing new skills to make your life run more optimally. Empowerment, similar to assertiveness, involves you enhancing your capabilities to make choices and to transform those choices into desired actions and outcomes. Importantly in this process, your actions build your confidence and improve your efficiency in your daily activities.

When you feel more empowered, the positive outcome for you is that you will have the freedom of choice and action. This will enable you to better influence the course of your life and have better control over the decisions which affect you.

The essence of empowerment, really relates to *Self-Determined Change*.

It's about increasing your personal development opportunities, improving your quality of life, and enhancing your personal development outcomes.

Empowerment Areas to Practice

There are many strategies that you can practice, though in my experience, there are certain elements that are almost always present when empowerment efforts are successful. The main elements of empowerment that underlie all personal change are:

1) Access to Information

2) Participation and Inclusion

3) Accountability

4) Organizational Skills

Access to Information

Always remember, "Information is Power". It's important to learn as much as you can about the situation you find yourself in and the possibilities and opportunities you have to gain knowledge, which may help you both short and long-term. *Why do you need information?* Remember, when you are informed, you have a better chance to take advantage of opportunities, exercise your rights, negotiate effectively and access relevant services that you may need. *So where can you get information from in this day and age?* Well, there is always the usual media forms, such as, television, newspaper, radio and more commonly now, the internet. Other areas which may provide you with information rather surprisingly are soap operas, poetry, discussions, debates and stories. We also have laws now that allow us more access to information should we need it. It's important that you don't underestimate your need for knowledge and information and where you can find it, because as I mentioned, "**Information is Power.**"

Participation and Inclusion

Empowerment is about you *participating* actively in your life and taking control over decisions and understanding the resources available to you. *Inclusion* is about including the right people in your life to help you gain knowledge and understand your priorities, which will provide you with a commitment to change.

Participating actively involves taking full responsibility for what you do and how, and not being in denial at any aspects of your behaviour. When you make decisions, it's important they are informed and blameless. What I mean by blameless is that, irrespective of how your decision turns out, you don't look to apportion blame on anybody else but yourself.

Including the right people in your life who are knowledgeable and who provide good counsel is important for you to learn new information and to provide you with improved ways of doing things.

Accountability

It's important for you in your life that if you seek change for the better, you are accountable for all aspects of your behaviour. In essence, it means that you are responsible for what you do and say, and if need be, you have to explain yourself. In terms of empowerment, the most important person you need to explain things to is, **Yourself!**

After all, if you are living a life where you apportion blame on others, and are not honest to yourself in terms of what you do and say, then how can you expect to learn, grow and become empowered? It's just not possible. By understanding the mechanisms that make you function, or make you fail, you can begin to work on and repair the flaws that may weaken you as a person or may weaken you in terms of providing you with the tools to improve your life.

Empowerment here equates to being accountable and responsible for your life, so that you can honestly see what you lack and then implement the necessary measures to provide you with the life-force that you need, instead of hiding behind blame and excuses.

Organizational Skills

Being organized and being able to organize people involved in your life is important with regard to empowerment because it provides you with the ability to work together with other people, to organise your life how you want it to be, and to mobilize your resources to solve any problems that may arise.

When you and your life are organized, you are more likely to make sure that your voice is heard and that your demands are met. Organisation provides you with structure in your life, together with a systematic approach and a sense of order.

Once you have developed and implemented your organisational skills into practical and integrative roles in your life, it allows you to focus on a higher level of development for you, a level of development that includes self-actualization and self-realization. An important aspect of this is that it provides you with the strength to make the necessary changes in your life.

Sometimes those changes can include:

- Ending a bad relationship

- Quitting a difficult job

- Chasing your dreams and goals

- Refusing to be downtrodden anymore

- Gaining the strength to stand up for your beliefs

Although the above areas to practice are separate, they are all connected to a degree and work together in synergy to help you gain the strength you need to move forwards in your life. In essence, they help to *empower* you.

As we have seen, changing and moving forwards in your in your life requires a certain, energy, force and power. The problem for most people is that they are stuck in a rut, or they procrastinate, or they suffer from severe inertia. If we analyze more closely the thoughts of people who are suffering from inertia, as opposed to those who are empowered, this is how it would look:

HOW WE THINK

Suffering Inertia:		Empowered:
Helplessness	>	Choice
Depression	>	Excitement
Paralysis	>	Action

The importance of feeling empowered, is that you have a healthier view of the world, you have the power to react in the correct manner to situations in your life, you have the power to do the necessary things to facilitate growth in your life, you have the power to create happiness and satisfaction in your life, you also have the power to behave appropriately and the power to love.

When you feel this kind of power in your day-to-day existence, you become self-reliant. Your life doesn't depend on what other people can do for you, or if you can get other people to do what you want them to do. Being empowered provides you with the ability to get *yourself* to do what you want to do. When you don't feel this way about yourself, you become dependent and you lose your sense of inner peace. This leaves you in a very vulnerable place.

Power fills you with positive energy and makes you feel more self-assured. By being more powerful within yourself, you will feel more authentic and true to yourself, and you will be more loving to the people in your life. In reality *power and love* go together. With power, you can develop a stronger sense of inner peace and not be afraid of relationships. With no power, love is distorted.

If you have any inner conflict between power and your ability to love or be loved, it's important you re-train your mind by creating new thought processes. Repeat to yourself twenty times each morning, afternoon and night time:

I AM TRULY POWERFUL AND I AM MUCH LOVED.
Also:
I AM TRULY POWERFUL AND I AM REALLY LOVING.

An empowering variation is:

I AM TRULY POWERFUL AND I ABSOLUTELY LOVE IT!

By repeating these positive statements to yourself, you retrain your brain to accept the ideas of power and love being compatible with each other, and you will feel more comfortable with this concept. After all, to have balanced relationships and inner peace, you need to understand the synergy between power and love. If you feel powerless, like a twig being tossed around in a sea of negativity, it will be hard for you to see the opportunities in your life and feel the love and positive energy that are around you.

To become more empowered in your life, you need to start with being *aware* of what situation you are truly in, then you need to take the necessary steps to forge ahead with your plans. Just by working out and understanding where you are in life, and then making a plan of action, can be very powerful tools, as they are the first steps in taking action. Always remember, ACTION IS A VERY POWERFUL TOOL! Once you feel motivated, you start heading in the right direction.

To help you feel motivated, it is important to conserve your energy and use it where you really need to. Learn to lighten up and not take yourself too seriously, and drop any excess emotional baggage that you are carrying around which will eventually wear you down. Also, as you head to where you need to be heading in your life, bear in mind that you will have your difficult days, and that there are always new experiences that will challenge your sense of personal power.

Always keep in mind the direction you want to be heading in, because it will help you make decisions in the *here and now.* Before you take the next step in your life, or the next course of action, learn to ask yourself:

"Is this next action moving me to a more empowered place?"

If the answer is "no", then you should really think twice about doing it.

Sometimes you may continue with an action knowing that it will eventually cause you more pain than happiness. If you do, it's important you don't berate yourself over this. Work out where you went wrong and take responsibility for your actions and their outcomes, so that in future you can take a different course of action that will bring you different results. It's important to use your "mistakes" as a learning experience so that you don't keep repeating them. Remember, each time you berate yourself for any course of action that you have taken and which you haven't learn from, you will ultimately not end up becoming stronger and more empowered.

A word of caution: Common courses of action people take where they are not satisfied with the outcomes and yet keep repeating the patterns are:

* Choosing the "wrong" types to get involved with in a relationship. The relationships never work out, yet some people never learn and keep choosing the same types over and over again.

* Starting different "fad" diets that work only short term. When they are unhappy with their weight again, they start another diet hoping for different results.

* Promising themselves to take better care of their health by cutting back on drinking or smoking, which they will do "when the time is right". However they continue to find excuses for continuing with their actions.

* Promising themselves not to get angry with friends, family and strangers, that maybe they will seek professional help for their problematic behaviour, but they continue getting angry with everyone and don't do anything about it.

Would you say any of the above scenarios apply to you? If they do, then you are stopping yourself from becoming empowered in various areas of your life and you will keep perpetuating the same mistakes.

When you strive to change for the better, it's important you use and trust your intuition to gauge how far you are progressing when you decide to take a positive course of action. Although to other people you may appear to be the same, it is your own sense of inner peace and growth that will determine how strong you become when it comes to eliminating certain negative traits and patterns of behaviour; thus enabling you to make the right future choices.

To help you on the path to empowerment, it's important you focus on your vocabulary when you are talking and thinking about things. Make sure that little voice in your head is not critical and negative because your use of words will have a tremendous impact on your quality of life. Certain words will have a destructive effect, while others will be more empowering … Choose your words wisely!

I have constructed a table below to illustrate this for you:

DESTRUCTIVE-TO-EMPOWERMENT VOCABULARY

DESTRUCTIVE	>	EMPOWERED
I can't	>	I won't
I should	>	I could
It's not my fault	>	I'm totally responsible
It's a problem	>	It's an opportunity
I'm never satisfied	>	I want to learn and grow
Life's a struggle	>	Life's an adventure
I hope	>	I know
If only	>	Next time
What will I do?	>	I know I can handle it
It's terrible	>	It's a learning experience

Before I analyze the table above in greater detail, I will point out that when I work with clients and we cover empowerment and look at the power of vocabulary in everyday thinking and speech, I always point out the following quote, which helps them to see the significance of vocabulary and self-belief.

"Whether you think you can, or think you can't – you're right."

Henry Ford

Psychologists love this quote (as do many other people!), because it sums up everything about confidence, self-belief, mindset and the idea that the words you choose to use, define your outlook and outcomes in life.

Let us go back to the use of vocabulary and how using certain words and phrases impact on your perceptions and the perceptions of other people of you.

"I can't" has the implication that you have no control over your life. It's best to delete its use from your vocabulary! When your subconscious hears the words "I can't", it believes what it hears and not what is true. Your own subconscious then perceives you as being weak, and that is registered and stored in your mind. Let us say you are asked to do something and you say, "I can't", because you want to get out of doing it. Your own subconscious will therefore register you as being weak. The truth of any situation where you say "I can't", is that either you can (and don't want to) or you are looking to do something else that has a higher priority for you. The only problem is that your subconscious can't discern the difference, and still recognizes weakness and registers you as being weak! When you say "I won't", it puts the situation into a realm of choice for you and therefore gives you the *power to choose* what you want to do.

When refusing to do something, it's best to be truthful, because truth indicates integrity, confidence and power. When you speak the truth, your subconscious hears you stating your priorities with definition and clarity, and the outcomes you choose serve your growth the best. Honesty means that you aren't a victim of circumstances and situations.

"I should" is also another expression that implies you are a victim with no choice. "I could" is a far more powerful expression to use. "I could visit my friend today, but I'm *choosing* to go shopping instead." This provides you with the power of choice, instead of obligation.

I *could* visit my friend or I *could* go shopping = Choice

Using the word "should" equates to obligation and can bring on a sense of guilt or a feeling of upset, which are both negative and draining emotions. Remember, you are not empowered when you use the word *should*.

Saying "It's not my fault" again shows you not taking responsibility for your actions and makes you look like a helpless victim of circumstance.

"It's not my fault I always pick losers."

"It's not my fault I failed the exam."

"It's not my fault I have no friends."

You can empower yourself by taking responsibility for your actions and therefore you might be able to see what you can rectify and improve on in the future. Whenever something goes wrong in your life, look at what *you* can do to prevent it from happening again. Responsibility means you are better prepared for the next time something happens and this means you are in a position of control in your life. A position of control then results in you having more strength and power in your life, which ultimately results in fewer worries and fears.

RESPONSIBILITY > CONTROL > EMPOWERMENT > FEWER FEARS

Another defeating and negative phrase is "It's a problem". However difficult it is, and sometimes it's extremely difficult, try to look for any positives and the opportunity to grow whenever life throws an obstacle or challenge your way. By saying "It's an opportunity", you allow yourself to face difficult situations in a possibly rewarding way. Each time you face a troubling or stressful dilemma, it presents you with an opportunity to find the strength to deal with it in a better way. *The better you deal with your problems, the more empowered you become.* This is very important because as we all know, life never runs smoothly and can be pretty unpredictable, however the only constant factor can be the way we deal with whatever life throws at us.

Let's look at the difference between "I hope" and "I know". When you say "I hope", it implies you have no control or power in a situation. You sound like a victim whose destiny depends on fate. "I know" sounds more powerful and exudes calmness and inner peace when you say it or think it.

Example:

"I *hope* my relationship works out well …"

"I *know* my relationship will work out well …"

If we now look at the difference between "If only" and "Next time", we will see the pattern following on. "If only" sounds resigned with no hope or control behind it. "Next time" sounds powerful because it implies you have gained knowledge and are prepared to use it the next time you encounter a similar situation.

Example:

"If only I had said that in the interview …"

This can become more powerful for you if you say:

"I've learned from my 'mistakes', and next time, I will make sure I say that in an interview …"

"What will I do?" is another question filled with hopelessness and resignation. You can hear the lack of control and fear in the words themselves. "I can't meet anyone special in my life. I don't want to be single forever. What will I do?" You can feel the desperation in a sentence like that. All of us have incredible resources of power within us, which we may not have drawn on before. When you say something like, "I'm sure I will meet the right person for me at some point in the future. Whatever happens to me in my life, I know I will handle it and succeed", you sound at ease with yourself and you sound powerful and in control of your life.

If you tend to see the world as terrible and the events that happen as terrible, and you frequently use a phrase like "It's terrible!" to emphasise this, then guess what, many things in your life will be *terrible*! Some things may just be an inconvenience for you, or they may be a little irritating, in fact many things are not terrible at all. The way you deal with many trivial things in your life teaches your subconscious mind that it is a drama, or horrible, or terrible, if you see it that way! Remember, your mind will register and store your very negative perceptions as being *your* reality.

As difficult as it may be, replace these fearful and negative expressions with, "It's a learning experience …" Even if something really bad happens in your life and you view it as "terrible", bear in mind that if you see it to be so, you take away *your* power to deal with the situation. Many people have gone through serious illnesses and bereavement and have come through the experience more enlightened and understanding of life.

If you have suffered a major illness, or the loss of a loved one, you will know that your life has changed irrevocably in many ways. After the pain and grief, you re-evaluate your thoughts, beliefs, friendships, and lifestyle and question every aspect of your existence. You value yourself and your loved ones even more so, and eliminate the negative emotional drains that you previously placed in your life. You redefine yourself and re-align your way of thinking: things that made you angry, stressed or resentful before, don't seem to be as important any more. You learn to let go of certain things and people, and feel a lot calmer in many aspects of your life. Sometimes it becomes an opportunity for you to express yourself and push yourself physically or emotionally in other ways, therefore you achieve things you never thought possible. All this can come about if you view extreme negativity and pain in your life as a true "learning experience". Sometimes unfortunately, you may have to experience a personal nadir before you get the opportunity for re-growth … But it only becomes an opportunity if you redefine your views and see it as an opportunity.

You can now see that even if something truly debilitating happens to you in your life, it doesn't have to represent an "end", but a new "beginning" where new opportunities and new possibilities await you.

Examples of what people have done in times of adversity:

* Started a charity

* Ran a marathon

* Learned to play a musical instrument

* Written a book

* Developed their artistic sides

* Learned a new language

* Started political campaigns

* Travelled extensively

* Done volunteer work

* Joined groups and associations

In fact these are just a few examples of how people have coped with personal adversity and used it as a "learning experience" to enhance their lives. So don't just sit there and say "woe is me", get up and go and do something positive to change your life!

It all starts with how you view yourself and your life, and the key here is to start by changing the way you think and speak. Although changing your vocabulary may seem trivial, it really is not. By deleting words such as 'problem, difficulty, struggle, can't' from your vocabulary, you change the way you see yourself and the way that you are seen by others. By displaying your inner strength and power, you will be treated differently by everyone. The more powerfully you speak, the more of a force you will feel and be in your environment. This all adds to your sense of *empowerment*.

Another way you can create more power in your life is by *Pushing Yourself to Your Limits*. What I mean here, is try to expand your life by doing things, however large or small, that take you out of your comfort zone. Don't be fearful of trying new things, because even if you 'fail', at least you have pushed yourself in some way to try something new. After all, at the very least you will gain a new impetus to try new things, and doing *something* is better than doing nothing, because:

DOING NOTHING = BEING POWERLESS

What is important to know, is that the more you expand your limits, the more powerful you become. As you keep pushing your limits and expanding them, you also expand your comfort zones. Your world of experience builds, as does your confidence, your inner strength and levels of power, which all result in you *growing* on every level.

An example of you continuing expansion and growth is:

- You decide to do a part-time art course after many years of not using your artistic skills. As you open up and become more receptive – learning more and developing your talent – you realize how good you really are. Your peers take notice of your art work and before long you are exhibiting your work. The local newspapers, radio and television stations start to take notice of what you're doing, and before you know it, your art work is lauded and *you* are being asked to make presentations and teach your own courses.

Each level of expansion here only happens because you have taken the first step to expand your skills, and ultimately, you continue to grow as it becomes easier and easier to push yourself and stretch your comfort zones.

It's important to keep pushing yourself and your limits because this eventually pushes you from left to right on the "Destructive to Empowerment Vocabulary" Chart.

The Importance of Visualization in Pushing Yourself to Your Limits

Visualize ~v. form an image of something in the mind.

Oxford English Dictionary

Every night before you go to bed, think over the activity you will be doing the following day which will push you to your limits. Close your eyes, and in your mind's eye, see yourself doing the desired activity. Make your visualization as clear as possible, and repeat it a few times until the image is anchored in your imagination and mind. As you go through the day, make a mental note of where you find yourself hesitating, and base your future visualizations at these 'points of hesitation'. If you can get through these points, then that's perfect, but if not, then in your next visualization session, imagine and see yourself going through the point where you were previously stuck at. So remember, the more you push yourself to your limits, and the more you stretch your comfort zones, the more empowered you become.

When you are aiming to move from destructive behaviour, thinking and vocabulary to a more empowered way of being, always remember to have integrity and love (both for yourself and others) behind ALL your actions. These ingredients are imperative in building your sense of self-worth, and a stronger sense of self-worth equates to empowerment.

INTEGRITY+LOVE+SELF-WORTH=EMPOWERMENT

It's important for you to understand and know that you already have more power in you than you could possibly have imagined. In this chapter I have looked at empowerment, what it means, and how certain techniques may help you, but in reality, the core message I am trying to get across to you is that, this *power and energy* is already inside you. It's just waiting to emerge and looking for the right channel to do so. It is more than sufficient to create a fulfilling, satisfying and joyful life for you. Maybe you haven't realised it previously, but it's just a question of knowing how to tap into your latent energy reserves.

What I have tried to do in my work as a psychotherapist (and the aim of my book) is to try to get people to understand they are all unique with special talents, and with the ability to develop themselves to become truly outstanding. The same applies to you. The only person stopping you doing what you want to do, is *you*! Don't blame anyone else. Don't even blame yourself... It's difficult to rid yourself of years of negative conditioning, but it's not impossible. Make a commitment to yourself and then stick to it. Read and re-read this book and other books that may help you. Speak to experts who can help you rid yourself of negative belief systems and help you to become empowered to do what you've always wanted to do. *It takes practice, belief and repetition for new and healthier ideas to take hold and become a part of you.*

We are all designed to innately use our talents, abilities and personal powers. When we don't, we feel hopeless, paralyzed, helpless and depressed. For us to achieve everything we were meant to, and create a wonderful and exciting life, we need to find the strength from within us. We need to *Empower Ourselves*.

"I was always looking outside myself for strength and confidence, but it comes from within. It was there all the time."

Anna Freud

CHAPTER FOUR:

ARE YOU A VICTIM?

"The wise man in the storm prays... Not for safety from danger, but for deliverance from fear..."

As we have seen so far, in our endeavors to become more assertive, empowered and rid ourselves of negative, fearful thoughts which hold us back, it is imperative that we are totally honest with ourselves. Too often in our lives we kid ourselves about how we feel and about our own level of culpability and responsibility for how our lives have turned out. Sometimes we continue with our negative belief systems and our self-defeating and self-destructive behaviors. In effect we become victims of our own thoughts and behaviors ... Are *you* a victim?

A major factor in thinking like a victim is that you blame everyone else for your shortcomings, apart from yourself. The ultimate problem here, is that this destructive way of thinking will inhibit your personal relationships and the quality of your life.

So what is the psychological journey of a person prone to this type of victimized thinking? It is quite difficult and complex to understand exactly the reasons behind this type of thinking. Many psychologists believe these belief patterns stem from childhood and could be a result of having highly critical parents or even mentally/physically abusive parents. Unfortunately, this can manifest itself in feelings of guilt and shame which can continue to develop into adulthood, and if left unchecked, can manifest into a continual "victim psychology". What does this mean? Well, a person with these thought patterns will continually blame other people in their lives, rather than deal with their feelings of guilt and shame, which will remind them of their childhood traumas.

So how can we define the thought patterns of an adult who displays "victim psychology?"

A person who is affected may be obsessed with fairness and what is morally or ethically right. In general, he or she believes that good things that happen in their lives are *deserved.* Anything bad that happens, is because someone else is being unjust, unfair, thoughtless, or even cruel. The real defining point for a person with the mentality of a victim, is that it is almost impossible for them to take *responsibility* for their part in a conflict or problem. The reason being that it may leave him or her feeling more vulnerable to feelings they struggle to deal with, such as:

- Feelings of Pain

- Feelings of Guilt

- Feelings of Shame

- Feelings of Fear

- Feelings of Rejection

These feelings may all come about because the person cannot accept responsibility for being wrong. From the outside, it may appear that a person displaying the patterns of a "victim mentality", may seem illogically self-centered, selfish and narcissistic. However, what is important to bear in mind is that it is actually an unhealthy and unfortunate reaction to deep-rooted traumatic pain, and it is not necessarily a conscious and inherent arrogance. What's even more unfortunate is that these behaviour patterns can be intolerable for other people, so personal relationships will no doubt suffer.

Victim psychology can have a vice-like grip on the sufferer and make it extremely difficult for them to make logical decisions. As a result, all their decisions are geared towards 'self-preservation' to its maximum level. They get so caught up in how unfair a situation is, that they are 'paralyzed' and find it extremely difficult to think of ways, actions, or possible solutions to overcome problems. Unfortunately, because a person suffering from *victim psychology* finds it difficult to fix problems, issues and arguments in their lives, they end up blaming and accusing everyone else but themselves. Again, this behaviour pattern has no redeeming feature and is ultimately destructive for all relationships.

Some people may be pre-disposed to have a tendency towards victim psychology and mentality. Certain situations in life may trigger this behavior. Dysfunctional relationships can lead to this type of thinking, even if there were no early, childhood traumas. For example, a person who is in a bad relationship with someone who has an addiction to drugs or alcohol, may have a legitimate complaint against the addiction, but they may end up using this addiction as a means of justifying their *own* passivity or interaction with their partner. What do I mean here? If the partner of an addict, began indulging in their own negative behaviors, such as going out extensively, or having affairs, they will end up blaming their partner's negative behaviour patterns for *their own* immoral or unethical behaviors. This is the type of behaviour pattern of a person who has victim psychology.

*They **justify** what they are doing wrong by **blaming** other people for **their own** weaknesses.*

The reality is that every person is responsible for his or her own behaviour and actions, irrespective of what their partner does or has done. Many people with victim mentality are involved in 'tit-for-tat' relationships, whereby they continually legitimize what they are doing by finding fault in their partners and then blaming them for their own actions. The old adage, "Two wrongs don't make a right", doesn't apply to them in their way of thinking.

Let's look at a couple of case studies and the problems that victim psychology creates:

* Adam has been married for two years. He has a good relationship with his wife and is close to his family, but has been struggling to cope with his wife's family, especially his mother-in-law:

"Dealing with someone who always sees themselves as the victim is really emotionally draining. Because nothing is ever their fault, they continually justify their bad behaviour by turning things around so that *they* become the victim!

My mother-in-law is a classic example of this type of person. I really don't enjoy spending time with her. I know it sounds like the classic 'mother-in-law' cliché, but she really is overbearing, manipulative and vulgar. Whenever she does something and upsets someone, she always manages to turn it around and finds fault with the other person, blaming them and saying it's all *their* fault! If anything is said back to her, she becomes defensive, says it's because she is not liked, and then uses emotional blackmail to manipulate the situation to her advantage! At work no-one likes her. If anything goes wrong, it's never her fault; she blames her colleagues, her bosses, her lack of training, the clients, EVERYONE but herself. I'm sure if they could fire her they would.

I blame her family for all this, especially her husband. My father-in-law is the classic 'enabler'. He panders to all her needs and runs after her trying to constantly please her. He never stands up to her and whenever she gets upset, he is so apologetic to her … it really is pathetic to watch."

Does Adam's mother-in-law sound like anyone you know? If you're being honest, does she sound like you in any way?

Looking in from the outside, Anya has a good life. She has a good job with a good salary, lives in a nice house, has a few close friends and enjoys the company of men (she is on many dating websites, has many lovers and non-serious relationships). So what can be wrong in Anya's life?

"My ex-husband is making my life hell. Everything is a constant struggle with him. Our divorce wasn't very amicable because he is so tight with his money. I had to fight tooth-and-nail to get a proper settlement, and even then I don't think he is paying me what he should be. If it were up to him, I would be living in a cheap apartment in a bad part of town. He is so unreasonable.

I was the one who wanted the divorce, but so what? It doesn't mean he shouldn't be taking good care of me and our daughter. He was so unresponsive to my needs in the marriage, that I was forced to look elsewhere for the love and affection that he should have been giving me. Our love life was not very good either. In many ways, he was to blame for me looking for love outside the marriage. If he couldn't satisfy me, then it's not my fault that I was driven into the arms of other men. I'm sure he wasn't being a hundred percent honest with me. I used to check his emails and phone, I couldn't find anything, but I'm sure he was either up to something behind my back or he had a secret bank account somewhere. Either way, he made me feel bad about myself.

Now he is being unreasonable when it comes to childcare. He should have our daughter every weekend to help me. I have an au pair and nanny, but that doesn't mean he shouldn't take more care of his daughter. My weekends are important for me, that's when I can go out and be with my friends and lovers. He needs to be a man and take care of his daughter. Life is *so* unfair sometimes."

Would you say Anya has a balanced view of her life? Is her experience of life a fair reflection of how she sees it?

Some people live in a constant state of anxiety because they feel that everyone and everything else in their lives need to change for them to be happy. It's never *their* fault. Sometimes people may need professional help to enable them to see the error of their ways. The only problem is that getting them to admit they need help is also a very difficult task. For If they do that, it may appear to them that they are weak, guilty or wrong, and the whole point of their behaviour is for them to avoid those feelings.

People come to see me for help in their lives, and I encounter all types of people from different cultures, backgrounds, age-groups, etc. These are some of the common complaints I encounter on a daily basis:

- People who complain about their ex-wives or ex-husbands

- People who complain about their work or bosses

- People who complain about being lonely

- People who complain about their marriages

- People who complain about single life

- People who complain about their children

- People who complain about lack of money

- People who complain about their lack of opportunity

- People who complain about everything

All these people are in some way playing the role of victim and not taking full responsibility for their experiences in life. They have given their power away to someone or something else, and when this happens, instead of feeling more empowered, they are suffering from pain, fear and inertia. Going back to my previous chart, instead of moving towards empowerment, they are remaining in the inertia/ destructive zone. As a result, they feel trapped and paralyzed and struggle to see a way out of their predicaments.

What I am saying is that if you think about it, when you are stuck in a loveless relationship that is not satisfying you; when you feel trapped in a monotonous and repetitive job that you hate; when you are dissatisfied at being single and are desperate for that special person to come into your life; when you feel let down by your family and friends; and when nothing in your life seems to be working out the way you want it to, you are playing the role of victim. And being a victim equates to being powerless and fearful.

It may be hard for you to see or understand the situation you are in, but what you must comprehend, is that on some level, you have chosen what is happening to you. All the things that are happening in your life are happening because you are allowing them to. You are giving them credence to be in your life. You are the common denominator for all the things which exist in your life. Is this now clear enough for you to grasp? *The only person sabotaging your life is you.* It's not your husband. Not your wife. Not your friends. Not your boss. Not your family. Not your children … *The only person sabotaging your life is you!*

On the highest level of Abraham Maslow's 'Pyramid of Hierarchy Needs' is self-actualization (Maslow stated that once our basic human needs were met, the top of the pyramid represented what our full potential is and the realization of that potential - "What a man can be, he must be".) Once we understand and gain the realization that we are responsible for all our difficulties, we understand that the solutions lie within us. However painful this realization and actualization process is for you, it becomes *an awakening* for you, an epiphany, that 'light bulb' moment you have been waiting for to illuminate the path ahead in life for you

"Not everything that is faced can be changed, but *nothing* can be changed until it is faced."

Lucille Ball

When I present the concept of being responsible in my sessions with clients, I present them with what I call "Rules of Responsibility". These rules keep them aware and mindful at all times of their thinking and behavior, and helps them to stay focused in their aims of taking more responsibility in their lives.

RULES OF RESPONSIBILITY

Rule 1

Never Blame Yourself:

This is an important concept, because although the idea of being *answerable* and *accountable* for your behaviour is the key to mastering the belief system of responsibility, it doesn't mean you have to be harsh and critical of yourself. Ironically, if you are too harsh and critical of yourself, it will have an adverse effect on you and it will be a self-defeating exercise. There is a fine line between understanding your own culpability to what happens in your life, and punishing yourself, being uber-critical and putting yourself down, because the over-riding message to yourself if you do that is:

"I'm not good enough. I keep failing and I'm useless. I just can't control myself. Will I ever learn from my mistakes?"

It's important not to be hard on yourself and understand that you have done your best throughout your life with the tools you had available at that given time. You are not critical of technology when you see that your mobile phone of five/ ten years ago doesn't have the capability and capacity of your phone today. The same should apply to how you view yourself. As you have continued to develop, new experiences and new adventures have added to who you are. Another important thing to understand is now that you are learning a new way of thinking, you will start to perceive things differently and start to change many of your future behaviors and actions. There is no reason for you to berate yourself or be regretful of your past behavior. As mentioned previously, it's all part of the learning experience for you. Maybe you have caused unhappiness in your life for yourself and others, but don't blame yourself and see yourself as being at fault. Remember, you are now moving forwards with greater enlightenment towards self-fulfilment. This 'journey' takes time and doesn't happen overnight, so just be patient.

Rule 2

Never Blame Anyone Else for Your Life's Misgivings

Apportioning blame on whatever level is a destructive mental state. Don't blame yourself (Rule 1) and don't blame other people (Rule 2). By blaming outside forces and factors for any of your life's misgivings, you continually give away your power and create fear, mistrust, pain and depression.

Sometimes people remain adamant that their suffering is because of someone else's behaviour and actions, but what is important to focus on and understand, is that you create what goes on in your head, not other people. This is a fundamental rule of psychology also. Just to repeat, until you understand that it is *you* who creates the thoughts in your head, you will never be in control of your life.

Here are some common complaints I hear in session, and the questions I have used to help challenge those beliefs:

Poppy: "Actually it's not my fault I get so down and depressed. Why did I have to get such a serious illness?"

Why are you always so stressed? Why are you so negative and angry all the time? Why do you drink so much alcohol? Why do eat so unhealthily? Why don't you use your illness as a defining point to change your life for the better?

Lana: "Actually it's all my husband's fault that I have been so unhappy and miserable during our marriage."

Why are you so consumed with anger because of his inability to communicate with you? Why can you not appreciate some of the good things he has done for you instead of continually finding fault with him? Why have you continued to remain in the marriage (if it's so bad)?

Hayley: "Actually it's not my fault that we have had a double-dip recession and I am stuck in a job that I hate."

Why are you not looking for the positives in having a job? Why can't you appreciate your position in such difficult times? Why are you not looking to improve your CV and apply for other jobs? Why can't you see that other people are managing to find jobs in such difficult times?

Lawrence: "Actually, if I didn't have any children, I wouldn't feel so trapped and I would be able to work and live abroad... It's my children's fault really."

Why haven't you noticed that other people with children seem to achieve their work goals? Why haven't you made more of an effort to bond with your children? Why don't you see your children as a blessing rather than a hindrance?

In all of the above instances, someone or something else is being blamed and held at fault for the angry, maladaptive and negative thoughts of these individuals.

Rule 3

Never Let Inertia and Procrastination Rule Your Life

This rule goes back to being assertive, being empowered and setting yourself attainable goals. When you are striving to achieve something you truly desire in your life, you are much more likely to take responsibility for what you do and how you do it.

- Look at yourself physically. Are you looking and feeling the way you want to? If not, then why aren't you doing what you need to do so that you create the body you desire. You must exercise (more) or adapt your diet to cut out the excess sugars and fats that increase your calorie intake. If you have time to sit and watch TV, then you have time to exercise and prepare healthy food!

- Look at the people in your life, your circle of friends and family for example. Whose company do you enjoy and who would you like to spend more time with? Why don't you text, call or send an email to them asking to meet up and spend more time together. Everyone is busy these days, but it only takes one person to make an effort. Let that person be *you*!

- We all want a nicer, bigger or better home, and one day hopefully we will get the house we dream of and work hard for, but until then, make the most of where you live now. Re-decorate, buy new furniture or accessories for your home. It doesn't take too much money or effort to create a calm, peaceful, and loving environment to live in. Making an effort leads to pride and that leads to greater responsibility.

Effort > Pride > Greater Responsibility

Most people spend their lives living in constant inertia and procrastination - waiting for the perfect job, waiting for '*the one*' to magically appear in their lives, waiting for other people to help them achieve, waiting for a big lottery win, etc., etc. There's no need to wait for anyone to provide you with anything in your life. There's no need to accept your lot in life, and then spend your life moaning and groaning about what hand fate has dealt you. YOU have the power to achieve what you need to in your life. It may take a little time, but be patient. With the magic ingredients of *desire, attainable goals, commitment, action* and *drive*, you can achieve anything you put your mind to!

Rule 4

Never Let That Negative Voice in Your Head Win

Unfortunately for most of us, what holds us back, criticizes us or puts us down (more than anything or anyone else), is that little voice in our heads. Our internal dialogue is responsible for how we view our environment. Many of us just think of it as our normal thought processes and some of us aren't even aware that it's there! For many people, the voice is unfortunately one of criticism, debilitation and disapproval-It's the one you hear in your head telling you that 'you can't, you're not good enough, you don't stand a chance, you shouldn't bother trying, you should give up' and so forth.

Examples of your negative internal dialogue are:

"Why haven't I heard back from my friend? It's been a few days since I sent her a text. I hate it when people don't respond back ASAP. It's a sign they don't care. I mean, how long does it take to send back an acknowledgement…? Actually, I'm always there for her when she has problems with her husband and children, she's quick to respond then. It's always like that when people want something; you can't get them off the phone, but when they're "busy" you don't hear from them! It's the same with my other friends. I'm always there for them in their hour of need, but who's there for me when I want someone to talk to. It really irritates me when people just leave you hanging after you contact them, and then they have the temerity to not apologize when you finally hear from them, as if nothing has happened. Sometimes they pretend they have forgotten, or pretend they have been *so* busy to get back to you, it really is annoying and disrespectful I find. Sometimes I wonder why I bother to have friends. I am the one who always makes the effort and makes all the plans, they just sit back and expect me to do everything. I must have "doormat" written across my forehead, because everyone has always taken liberties with me. Maybe I should call up my friend and ask her what she is playing at. I think it's time I confront a few people about their bad behaviour and lack of respect …"

Another example:

"I know we have been out on just a couple of dates now, but you would think he would show a little more interest in me. It's always me contacting him first and waiting for him to respond. Actually, when I think about it, I find that all men are like this. If you play it cool you don't hear from them, and if you call or text them, then they back away. I hate this 'dating game'. Why can't you just meet honest people who don't play games with you? I always wonder if I do or say the right thing; after all, I want to come across as cool and sophisticated, and not as a clingy and needy person. I really struggle when I don't hear back from men. I end up thinking even more about them, wondering what they are doing, and then imagining all sorts of negative scenarios where they are out with other women. I know I should be cool and act as if I don't care, but how do you do that? It must be me, I mean, I always pick the wrong types anyway. I am attracted to bad boys because I find them more attractive and interesting. Nice guys are dull and boring. Anyway, I'm going to contact this guy and let him know how I feel. I'm sick and tired reading about him on social media sites and finding out what he's doing, when he still doesn't have time to contact me. I need some answers because this is just driving me crazy …"

These examples of what people think may resonate with you in some way, or you may have good examples of your own. After all, your own internal dialogue may be just as bad (or worse!) as in the above examples. Maybe that is why you may struggle to be alone or to have silence around you. If you feel the constant need to play music, watch TV, listen to the radio, be on the internet, etc., it could be a sign that you struggle to deal with your own thoughts, especially that little voice in your head. The one that is constantly self-critical, negative and self-deprecating.

Although you would think your internal dialogue operates for your own advantage constantly, unfortunately you could be stuck with your very own 'frenemy' who is with you 24/7. ('Frenemy' is a portmanteau word joining 'friend' and 'enemy' and implies that you have an enemy pretending to be your friend. In this instance, your enemy is your very own internal dialogue, who is a part of you and yet works to sabotage everything you do!)

Be mindful that your very own internal dialogue is making you a victim and keeping you down. In real life you wouldn't hang out with enemies, so make sure you are always aware of your thoughts and keep your *internal enemies* at bay by committing yourself to changing those negative voices into positive, caring and loving ones. Once you master this (and we will look at doing this in greater detail later on in this book), you will be able to enjoy your own company and attain the level of *inner peace* that will benefit you.

Rule 5

Never Ignore Your Emotional Triggers

Don't be a martyr in your life to all the emotional triggers that you perceive to be behind your reasons for feeling the way you do. If you are constantly creating scenarios in your life that give you the opportunity to 'gripe and groan' about your family, friends, jobs, partners, etc, then you are remaining powerless and perpetuating your role as victim. Every time you are waiting for someone else in your life to make you happy, you are not taking the responsibility you need to in order to make *yourself* happy.

Let us say you are angry at your partner for some reason, it's important to be mindful of what you are feeling and why. Ask yourself: "What am I unsatisfied with in my life that I should be dealing with, which is making me blame him (or her)?" This is a very important question that you should be focusing on and using in your life every time you get angry with other people (especially those 'nearest and dearest'). Maybe in your life, you are feeling depressed for some reason, or you are feeling a little insecure about something, or maybe you are worried about your finances; whatever it is, you may be taking it out on the person closest to you. On some level, you must know this is unfair behaviour and that you are deflecting your negativity onto your partner, so that he or she can "make it better" for you. When you behave like this, you become the victim again who is not being responsible for your own actions.

There is no such thing as 'Mr. Perfect' or 'Miss Perfect' in this world, always bear in mind that each and every one of us has our own issues that we are dealing with, so it's important you learn to deal with your own. Of course with your partner, you can work through difficult things together, but would it be fair of you to expect another individual to be your *saviour* and rescue you from any of the problems *you* have created? Of course it wouldn't!

A good relationship does of course involve nurturing each other, caring for each other, and supporting each other through difficult periods in life, but when you are not being responsible for yourself in any way, no amount of nurturing, caring or support from your partner will ever be enough for you. You become an 'emotional leech' in your relationship, draining your partner and then *blaming* him or her because it is never enough for you.

By all means, if your partner is not really providing you with the basic needs that are required in a well-functioning relationship, it is your responsibility to move on and find a more compatible partner for yourself. However, a word of warning is that it is important for you to work out if your partner really is as "terrible" as you perceive him/her to be, or is it more of a case of you *deflecting* your negativity onto him or her, and then blaming them for the shortcomings that *you* really suffer from.

How do you know when you are taking responsibility in your relationship?

When you reach the correct level of maturity to be in a relationship, you will naturally want the best for your partner. Their happiness makes you happy, their dreams and hopes become yours, and together you strive to accomplish shared goals. The most important factor is that you are not angry at your partner and you realise it is a choice for both you and him/her to be in a relationship. Your efforts to make the relationship work should also be reciprocated in every way, and are an indicator to the levels of responsibility that you both have. Always remember that every time you get angry, it is your determinant that you are not taking responsibility for yourself or the relationship.

Personal relationships are only one area where you may be a victim and feel powerless. Look at all the other areas of your life to work out if you're not taking responsibility. Any one of the following emotional triggers will indicate if things aren't going as they should be. Be careful every time you feel any of the following emotions:

- Anger

- Vengeance

- Self-pity

- Helplessness

- Intimidation

- Lack of Desire

- Jealousy

- Hopelessness

- Pain

- Disappointment

- Addictive Behaviour

- Upset

- Envy

- Blaming Others

- Lack of Focus

- Obsessive Behaviour

There are of course many other emotions that can be added to the list. Whenever you feel any of these negative emotional triggers, it is vital that *you* determine what *you* are not doing in *your* life that makes *you* feel these emotions. Once you do that, you can take full responsibility for what you are doing, and then take the necessary steps to rectify what is really wrong in your life.

Rule 6

Never Ignore Your Psychological Payoffs

You may have heard of a 'Psychological Payoff'. This simply means that whatever we choose to do in our lives, or however we choose to behave, there is a "payoff" for our behaviour. We always get back something for what we do. We may not be aware of what we get back, but we get back *something*, otherwise we wouldn't do what we do. Your payoffs are what perpetuate your behaviour patterns. Once you work out what your personal payoffs are, your behaviour patterns will make much more sense to you.

To help you understand yourself, and what 'makes you tick', we will firstly look at some examples of other people and see what their payoffs are.

* John was from a traditional Catholic background. He was fairly religious and old fashioned in many ways. He had separated from his wife a couple of years earlier, with whom he had a son and daughter. He met a new woman whom he wanted to marry, but despite being thirty-two years old, he found it difficult to tell his wife he wanted a divorce. When his new partner explained how angry and disillusioned she had become, John still had difficulty telling his wife and children he wanted a divorce. His new partner finally gave John an ultimatum, and this forced him to confront his issues. He found a therapist who helped him see that he was behaving as a "victim" because he believed his wife would make his life unbearable, his children would disown him and his parents would be devastated if he ended up divorced. This was what John truly believed and it left him feeling ashamed of himself and feeling extremely guilty.

Receiving the help that he desperately needed, John was able to see that his biggest problem actually related to his fear of letting go. Even though he was in a new relationship and no longer loved his wife, she represented a psychological "home to come back to", and he was fearful of permanently cutting that connection in his mind. This was in fact his psychological payoff for remaining in this state of limbo.

Once John fully understood his behaviour and his payoff, he began divorce proceedings against his wife. Actually, he found out that his wife hadn't planned to make his life unbearable, the children didn't disown him, and his parents were not devastated by his impending divorce.

Result: John recognised his payoffs were to blame for his procrastination and were his reasons to remain in the marriage. Once he understood this, his feelings of shame and guilt disappeared and he was able to move forwards and take action.

Another example:

* Martina was always feeling ill. She always had one complaint after another, and she was always arranging to see her doctor for "tests". Unfortunately for her, this interrupted many things she wanted to do with her life and in her life. She saw herself as being weak both physically and mentally. The interesting thing in this case was that when Martina was asked by her therapist what payoffs she had for her constantly being ill, she couldn't think of any!

The therapist ended up pointing out to her that being ill got her a lot of attention and it kept her in her comfort zone of feeling vulnerable and not having to take any risks in her life. Of course, for some time she denied this, until she could finally see there was credence to what was being said.

Martina *never* saw herself as being manipulative. However, when she was asked about her actions and consequences, she admitted that on a subconscious level, she knew what she was doing. When she was a child, illness was the only device that got her any attention from her mother and father. She then understood that in fact, she had been *creating* her illnesses which were in great part psychosomatic.

Result: When Martina became aware of her psychological payoffs, she started to make many changes in her life to create a different pattern of thinking.

She asked her family and friends to ignore her when she 'became ill', and to reward her for being positive and feeling well. She changed her diet and also joined a gym. She used motivational psychology to help push her to create and achieve new goals in her life. By understanding her payoffs, Martina was able to ask herself and answer the following questions:

"Do I want to continue getting attention for being ill for the rest of my life?"

"Do I want to find a more satisfying way to relate to people in my life?"

"Do I want to be an observer or a participant in my life?"

From these two case studies, you can see the influences that payoffs have in our lives. You may need help from a counsellor or therapist if you can't find the payoffs that are inhibiting you in your life. This is because usually, other people may see things from the outside a little more easily and quickly than you can. Once you learn what your deeper, psychological payoffs are for your behaviour patterns, you will be able to make the necessary changes to stop yourself continuing the behaviors that are holding you back in life.

Rule 7

Never Forget All the Choices You Have In Your Life

The important thing to always remember and bear in mind is that you always have the choice to work out and implement the paths you choose to take in life. ***How you choose to see your world, creates the world you see***. If you want to create the perfect body, then go out and achieve your goal. If you want to start-up your own business, then go out and achieve your goal. If you want to change your life outlook from negative to positive, then go out and achieve your goal. In fact, whatever you want to achieve in your life, the only person who can make that happen is *you*. The choice is yours. As you go through every day, it is important to realise that at every moment you are choosing how you feel. Whenever you encounter any difficult situation, learn to tune into your mind and ask yourself, "The choice is mine. What do I choose?"

Then think of your options:

- "Do I choose contentment or misery?"

- "Do I choose to see abundance or scarcity?"

- "Do I choose to see my own security, or do I choose to get angry at other people in my life?"

- "Do I choose to go after my goals, or do I choose to procrastinate indefinitely?"

Choose the option that allows you to become enlightened and grow as a person. There are many possible scenarios that you will encounter in your life which you may find difficult or challenging to handle. However difficult it may be for you to stay in control of your emotions, it is imperative you stay focused and understand your choices. Taking full responsibility for your actions and your life is a long and difficult process, but ultimately, a rewarding one.

Now that you understand the choices in life are yours, you have the power to always move to the up-side of any given situation. Your goal is a more satisfying life in whatever you do; this is irrespective of how other people may behave in your life. Remember, you are not responsible for *their* behaviour, you are only responsible for *your own* behaviour and actions. Once you understand this, you will feel a huge weight lifted off your shoulders as you finally understand your happiness lies entirely in your hands.

Here are some practical exercises to help you become responsible for your feelings and actions:

Exercise 1

Become more aware of what you say when you are speaking to, or about other people. Be mindful of the words you use and if you are complaining too much or using negative words. If you find you are constantly being overly critical about other people, try to use these situations to see if you can learn something new about yourself. You may be surprised at *your* motivation for behaving the way you do.

For example: When you are criticizing or making snide remarks about other people, is this because deep-down you really see yourself as the victim? Or is the real reason for your critique that it leaves you 'feeling superior' in some way when you 'put down' other people? Either way, long term you will struggle to take responsibility in your life if you are constantly focusing on *other* people in a negative manner. Be aware of what you are doing and why!

Exercise 2

Focus on the "gifts" you have received in your life from all the situations you have perceived as bad previously. Always remember that *something good comes from something bad.*

For example: After a relationship break up, you may be feeling hurt and in pain, but despite this, do your best to focus on all the good things you did together, and the positive things the relationship taught you. Try not to be negative and think things like "all my relationships end badly, people are so unreliable nowadays and they keep letting me down…" Learn more about *yourself* and what you truly want. If you aren't 'catching the fish you truly want to catch, try fishing in a new pond.' In other words, to get something new, you have to try and do something new (or different)!

Also, think of all the good and positive things that can come about from being single, such as developing new contacts and friendships in your life; having the freedom to do what you want to do; being able to travel wherever you want to go to; learning to be more self-reliant and self-sufficient; being more in control of yourself and less dependent on others, and so on.

Exercise 3

In a notepad, or on your phone/PC/tablet, or in your diary, write down all the choices available to you, so that you can change presently upsetting situations into positive ones.

For example: Let us say you have a friend who you think disrespects you in some way. His/her behaviour always leaves you feeling frustrated and angry. What choices do you have/could you make in this scenario?

You could stop seeing this friend. You could learn to be more light-hearted and make more jokes to diffuse your friend's indiscretions. You could talk to your friend about his/her behavior and how it makes you feel. You could become more like your friend and give back as good as you get… The key here is to do *something* rather than getting angry about the situation. Stop blaming others for your anger and upset. It is not about condoning the behaviour of other people, but more about you learning not to constantly be *reactive* and react negatively to your environment. What happens when you get angry? Your blood pressure rises, you suffer breathlessness and heart palpitations, you may get dizzy etc., whilst the other person is oblivious and happily carries on in their ignorance. So is it worth it? Of course it isn't!

In every situation you face, there are at least twenty – thirty ways to change your point of view. It's important that you understand this and that you try to make note of it in a lighthearted way. Whenever you encounter a situation that evokes an emotional response in you, think of *all* the possible points of view you can create for that situation. That way, you will see your 'normal' responses and views aren't etched in stone, you can be more flexible in how you view your environment. The choice *is* yours!

Exercise 4

Make a mental note of all the payoffs that keep you stuck in certain areas of your life. Ask yourself: "What comfort do I get from being like this? What images do I continually hold on to? What is it that I am avoiding? What is it that I am trying not to face?" Be as honest as you can with yourself as you search for the answers. Many times in our lives, we work on our 'default settings', we never question what we do, we just 'get on with it'. The point of this exercise is to make you become aware of what you do and why, which in turn will allow you to change your behavior patterns to healthier ones.

Exercise 5

Make a list of all the options you have in any given day. What I mean here is that when you are confronted with a difficult scenario, write a list of all the possible ways that you can behave and feel about it. Then practice the following visualization techniques:

Picture yourself happy about it; then sad about it; then feeling terrible about it; then feeling outraged by it; then being humored by it, and so forth. This will then show you that you have the capacity to change your views, and ultimately your feelings, when *you* choose to.

So each time you get angry for example, be mindful of the alternatives that you have. Make sure you don't put yourself down for being angry, and be aware this is a step for you to take responsibility for your anger, and to behave in a more optimal way.

<u>Exercise 6</u>

This exercise goes back to *controlling* that negative, little voice in your head. If you are prone to being critical, then this one will be difficult for you (though not impossible). Try to go one week without complaining about *anything*, and by not being critical of *anyone*! This will be difficult on three fronts:

1 – Realizing how much you complain and criticize on a daily basis.

2 – Realizing how much negativity envelops you on a daily basis.

3 – Realizing how difficult it is for you to actually *stop* being so negative and critical on a daily basis.

The biggest problem for you could be the interactions in your life. You may have inadvertently created a 'Sour Grapes Club' where your relationships are defined by how much moaning and putting down of others you do in your daily discussions.

Be careful that your, "Have you heard …? Did you know …? Why is she …? I don't think he … I doubt whether they …" and so on type of conversations are not all geared towards criticizing, bemoaning or gloating over other people. If they are, you really need to re-focus yourself and find a more harmonious and satisfying way of communicating.

Résumé: How to Stop Being a Victim and Regain Responsibility in Your Life

1. Stop blaming yourself for not taking responsibility and being in control. Always remember that you are continually doing your best and that all your positive actions are leading you to become more empowered.

2. Stop blaming other people and outside factors for the negative thoughts that you are harboring about your life. Only *you* can control *your* thinking, *your* actions and *your* behaviour.

3. Work out what you want in your life and 'go for it.' Stop waiting for other people to help you or hand it to you. You will end up waiting a long time!

4. Understand that your worst enemy is *you*! You have to defeat that negative, little voice in your head. Use this book (and others like it) or work with a professional to help you defeat, overcome or control it.

5. Be mindful of where and when you choose to play the role of victim. Tune into your thoughts so that you know when you're not being responsible for what you feel, what you have, what you say, what you do and what you are!

6. Work out what it is in your life that keeps you "stuck" where you are. Once you find your payoffs, you can work with yourself so that you will eventually become "unstuck".

7. Your life is always about choices. Understand them so that you can better control your behaviour, actions and feelings in any given situation. Always choose a 'win-win' scenario that leaves everyone in your life feeling happy and positive. This will lead you to a calmer life and leave you acquiring a sense of inner peace.

8. Finally, understand that whatever your religious beliefs may be, or whatever your levels of spirituality may be, you are only here *once* as you now are, at *this* given time. Your life is not a dress rehearsal, so: **Be Confident; Feel Empowered; Stop being a victim and take control of your life *now*!**

"Confidence and Empowerment are cousins in my opinion. Empowerment comes from within and typically it's stemmed and fostered by Self-Assurance. To feel Empowered is to feel free and that's when people do their best work. You can't fake Confidence or Empowerment".

Amy Jo Martin

CHAPTER FIVE:

POSITIVE THINKING!

"The way we choose to see the World, creates the World we see …"

B. N. Kaufman

There have been many books written over the years on Positive Thinking and how it can benefit you. In psychotherapy, a large part of it is based on your preconceptions of negativity and positive thinking, and how your beliefs, behaviors and cognition of them perpetuate your outcomes. The aim of this chapter is to condense many of the ideologies of positive thinking, and look at some techniques that you can practice to change your mindset to a more positive one. In essence, it is important to bear in mind that a positive and happy person is not the result of a certain set of circumstances, but rather he/she is the result of a certain set of attitudes. After all, it is your *attitudes* and *outlook* that will determine how you cope in life and if you're able to "*always look on the bright side of life*".

Many times in our lives negativity is a more 'normal' way to view the world. If someone seems overtly happy or positive, we may even think of them as being abnormal, weird or even 'having a screw loose!' Be honest, if you were walking down the road and you encountered a person who was smiling and grinning, would you think of that person as having something wrong with them? Would you find it more acceptable if they looked a bit miserable or down in the dumps? (This example applies more so to towns and cities, not smaller places where people tend to know each other!)

We seem more sympathetic and empathetic to people who seem negative because "we all have struggles", "everyone is having a hard time" and "life can be really tough sometimes". We accept this as being the 'norm'. All people have relationship, money, family and work problems, don't they?

Statistically speaking, the majority of what we worry about will *never* happen. We are in reality stressing over a <u>small</u> minority of the situations that we are envisaging as coming true. As this is factually correct, then does it not stand to reason that we should ALL be a lot more positive than negative? Our automatic assumptions are that being negative is *realistic* and being positive is *unrealistic*! Maybe the real point here is not about what we see as being realistic or unrealistic, but rather, "*Why are we choosing to be negative and miserable, when we can just as easily choose to be positive and happy?*" Think about it. There is no logical or statistical reason for you to choose negative thinking over positive thinking, and yet for the vast majority of us, that is our natural *status quo.*

As mentioned, attitudes and outlook are the main contributors to our way of thinking, so let's look at a couple of examples of this.

(Unfortunately, we may all suffer bereavement, divorce, retirement, redundancy, etc. at some point in our lives, but how we cope with adversity ultimately defines us).

* Dennis retired six months ago. He spent the years before his retirement dreading the day he would stop working. He delayed his retirement for as long as he could, because for him, his whole identity and understanding of who he was, was connected to his job. He made no plans for his retirement and saw it as 'the end' for him. He had no hobbies, no desires and no goals for his retirement. He always struggled to enjoy his free time and saw his retirement as a punishment. His wife

continually complained to him about his defeatist attitude and lethargy. His negativity became a 'self-fulfilling prophecy' for him. Because he saw his life as being worthless, his thoughts and actions reinforced this, and created this as his reality. His negativity created his "realistic" life of misery.

* Alan retired six months ago. He spent many months before he stopped working planning what he would do once his work life was over. Together with his wife, he made a list of all the places he wanted to visit, he bought many of the books he had always wanted to read, he enrolled on a language and art course, he started going out and socializing with new people, he started to do some volunteer work in the local community and he went for long walks in the country every few days with his wife. Although he had loved his job and missed working, he understood that *everything* in life has a limit, including life itself. He wanted to use his free time as optimally as he could and planned to grow and expand as a person in a way that was not possible while he was busy engaged in his work role. His positive outlook created a very "realistic" life of satisfaction and happiness.

Alan always brought a sense of optimism and exuberance to his work life, which he was now able to carry over into his retirement. The way he turned his negative experience of retiring from a job he loved into a positive triumph inspired many of Alan's colleagues as they also encountered the same situation as he had. It's important to adopt Alan's positive thinking because it shows that nothing is realistic or unrealistic, the only reality of a situation is our perception of it.

Always remember: *We Create Our Own Reality.*

The importance of positive thinking in our lives is that whenever we feel pain, apprehension, fear or other such negative emotions, we will then be able to move to a position of power.

In the above examples, although Dennis and Alan both had their worries, concerns and fears about retirement, Dennis

117

continued to hold onto his and it defined his retirement. For him it represented stagnation and misery. Alan on the other hand used his powers of positive thinking to create growth and expansion in his life.

Retirement is just one area in which positive thinking has created motivation, excitement and inner peace from a position of relative fear and apprehension. Without doubt, *positive thinking will pull you closer to finding your own inner powers.*

What is important for you to realise about your subconscious mind, is that it believes without prejudice whatever words you use to describe yourself and the position you find yourself in. Using positive words to describe yourself physically and emotionally results in you actually becoming *stronger.* If you use words like, "I am great, I am worthy, I am strong, my life is my responsibility, my life is what I make of it, everything will work out well for me ..." your subconscious mind will believe it and strive to create it as your outcome and reality.

The same applies if you use negative words, "I am depressed, I am unworthy, I am weak, my life is out of my control, everything will work out badly for me ...", again, your subconscious mind will believe it and strive to create it as your outcome and reality.

The incredible aspect of this, in a psychological sense, is that it doesn't matter if we actually *believe* these words or not, the mere use of these words in our vocabulary will make our subconscious mind accept and believe them. Whatever you feed your subconscious mind, it will create for you. *This is a very powerful concept to understand, so be extremely careful how you view yourself together with the words you use ...*

Positive thinking is not of course a new concept. Over the years many books have been written about the subject. All these books are still available today from people who popularized the ideology, people such as Norman Vincent Peale, Dale Carnegie, Napoleon Hill, Thomas Troward, Genevieve Behrend and Maxwell Maltz, to name but a few.

One thing that comes across in books, counselling and therapy is that positive thinking is *an ongoing process*. It isn't something that happens once in your life and that's it. It's not permanent. You constantly have to be mindful of how you are thinking and you have to keep practicing at being positive. Like any skill, if you don't practice it, you will lose it. You have to recognize that to remain positive, you need ongoing commitment, dedication and continued *practice*. Maybe people don't understand this, and as a result, either they don't understand what is involved and required, or they don't understand the natural peaks and troughs of human nature. **This means that positive thinking is a *continual* process that needs to be *continually* worked on.**

The way you have to look at it, is that it can be compared to physical exercise. You wouldn't work out to a peak physical level for yourself and achieve the body you wish for and then *stop,* would you? If you did, you would lose your stamina, your muscle tone, your strength, and so on. The same applies to positive thinking; you have to keep at it in order to maintain it.

The same rule follows with regard to your mental sharpness. When you use your intellect every day, working out problems, having discussions and stimulating your mind, it remains sharp. After a holiday, where you spend your time relaxing and doing nothing for a couple of weeks or so, your mental skills are compromised. You feel slower, a bit groggier, and mentally not as quick. It may take you a few days or even weeks to get back to your previous levels of sharpness.

Clearly then certain areas of ourselves, physically and mentally, need constant reinforcement. Maintaining your positive mental attitude is just one of these areas that need continual work.

The way you have to look at it is that every day, without thinking, you get showered, have a shave or put your make-up on, you dress smartly for work, you eat and drink, and do many other things without thinking as part of your daily routine. These are part of your necessities and daily personal habits that you have created for yourself. It would be a good idea for you to incorporate positive thinking techniques, quotes, ideas and actions into your daily routine to create *new* habits for yourself.

* Definition of a 'Habit'- **1**. Generally, a learned act. Originally the reference was to motor patterns, physical responses; this limitation is no longer recognized and perceptual, cognitive, affective habits are commonly cited.

2. A pattern of activity that has, through repetition, become automatized and fixed and is easily and effortlessly carried out.

Dictionary of Psychology, Penguin Reference

So now you know that creating new habits is a major factor of creating and implementing positive thinking, what happens when you hit a 'rough patch' and are enveloped in those debilitating negative thoughts? Well, just as you would start a diet and exercise regime to lose weight and tone up, you would also need to *take action* and implement a new mental regime to re-educate and retrain your mind.

What tools can help you?

1). Inspirational/Positive quotes - We are all touched by various quotes which may relate to us personally. Whatever quotes you find that work best for you, write them down or print them out. Place them all around you in your home and work place even, so that you are constantly reminded of something that inspires you and re-focuses your thought patterns. Sometimes in life our circumstances may change, different quotes may inspire us at different times, so try to update your quotes to relate to what you need at that given time.

Some good quotes for example are:

"Don't wait. The time will never be just right." – Napoleon Hill

"Do just once what others say you can't do, and you will never pay attention to *their* limitations again." – James R. Cook

"Success isn't something that just happens. Success is learned, Success is practiced and then it is shared." – S. Anderson

"You will never change your life until you change something you do daily." – Mike Murdoch

"The greatest glory in living lies not in never failing, but in rising every time we fall." – Nelson Mandela

"No act of kindness, no matter how small, is ever wasted." – Aesop

"The time is always right to do what is right." – Martin Luther King Jr

2). Self-help books – Books/ E-books like this one are designed to make you think, make you question, make you re-evaluate and finally change any behaviors and thoughts that are inhibiting you in your life. You can keep books permanently with you and have inspiration at hand whenever you feel you need it. It may not always be possible for you to see a counsellor or therapist, either in terms of your time or your finances, so the next best thing is an inspirational book. With technology today the way it is, there are also many mediums for you to find and download the relevant information that you need to help you stay positive.

3). Affirmations - What exactly is an Affirmation? It is a *positive statement that something is happening in the here and now*. It's not about the past and not about the future, but the present. It's a 'self-talk' tool at the highest level and also the easiest and cheapest to use for you.

Here are a few positive affirmations for you:

I am filling my life with peace and tranquility.

I am now dealing with all my worries and fears.

I am now creating a healthy and toned body.

I am now allowing myself to let go and be calm.

I am now filling my life with joy and abundance.

I am breaking old thought patterns and moving forwards in my life.

Please remember the following things about affirmations:

Affirmations are *always* in the *present*:

*I am **now** dealing with all my fears.*

*I am **now** facing and handling all my problems.*

Affirmations are *always* stated in the *positive* (not in the negative):

I am becoming stronger every day.

I am becoming more self-assured every day.

The affirmations you use should relate to you in your present situation- They will change as your emotions, mood and situations also change in your life.

How does all this relate to *you*?

We touched on that 'negative, little voice' that you may have earlier in this book, and in essence, everything in this chapter relates to how you deal with that voice. Once you have mastered taming that 'voice in your head', positive thinking will be a much easier concept for you in your day-to-day living. A simple way to understand the whole ideology of it is to see it as **BREAKING THAT NEGATIVE VOICE!** Everything in your power, should be geared towards that.

Some tips to help you create more positive thinking in your day-to-day life:

1). As obvious as it may sound, it's important to begin your day in a positive manner... Many of us wake up dreading the morning and the day ahead. Instead of that, try waking up to your favourite music, so that you are already singing along or dancing first thing in the morning. The power of music is very underrated; it engages all your senses at the same time and increases the levels of dopamine in your brain. (Dopamine is the chemical that sends "feel good" signals to the rest of the body and plays a vital role in motivation.)

You can also start your day to any motivational CD or download that inspires you. Lie in your bed with your eyes closed for fifteen – twenty minutes and let the soothing and positive messages sink in and become a part of your thought processes.

2). Continue with the positive start to your day by reading positive quotes and phrases (remember, you should have these placed around your home on cards, notes or even available on your mobile phone, tablet or PC).

3). During the morning, while you listen to some upbeat music, repeat your positive affirmations for the day. Before any negative voices have time to 'speak' to you, repeat your positive affirmations (preferably in front of a mirror for five – ten minutes). Believe in yourself and trust that repetition will, with practice, drown out the negative voices in your mind. Eventually, when you wake up, your 'default' mode will be positive and not negative.

Remember, positive thinking is a habit. Change your habits in the morning, from anything negative to positive. Avoid the news until later in the day and try not to read any negative stories in the newspapers. Or you can start your day with reading positive, self-help books like this one. Anything that gets you thinking in a positive and constructive way is advisable. Once you are feeling happier and much more positive in the mornings, you can revert back to some of your previous habits, however, what you will find is that when you encounter any sad or bad news, you will be more understanding and constructive in dealing with it, rather than being negative as you previously were.

4). Try to incorporate exercise, yoga or pilates into your daily routine in some capacity. If you have ten minutes in the morning try to do something physical to get your heart pumping and the adrenalin flowing throughout your body. After a little activity, endorphins are released which help you feel better and create a sense of well-being.

Note: If you don't have ten minutes in the morning to exercise or stretch, then get up ten minutes earlier!

5). As you travel to work in the mornings, use the commute as a time to perpetuate positive feelings. If you drive, then listen to upbeat music, or listen to positive and inspiring CDs or downloads. If you take trains or buses to work, again you can use your time optimally by reading motivational material: books, magazines, etc. Always remember, *you can listen to motivational downloads as you take that daily commute to and from work if you have no other time available to you.* In actual fact, it's probably a very good time for you to zone into those positive thought processes you want to create for yourself.

6). Your workplace should have some positivity attached to it. Whether you work in an office, salon, restaurant, garage or wherever, try to have some personal touches that relate to you/your happiness attached to it. These could be photographs, images or positive quotes that help keep you focused and feeling good throughout the day.

7). A good idea for you during the day is to read over your positive affirmations. You can have these on your phone, tablet, PC, diary, or even have them written on cards and notes in your pockets, bags, or around your home/ workplace. These will continually provide your mind with the 'training' it needs to stay positive. Remember, just like your body, your mind has to constantly be trained to remain positive, and being surrounded by positive affirmations is a good way to do this.

8). Throughout the day, you may be tempted to be drawn back into negative thinking and emotions. If this happens, keep your positivity levels high by giving yourself a positive 'boost'. Seek out *anything* that you *know* to be positive and will make you happy. Read something positive, listen to something positive, speak to people you *know* to be positive, repeat positive affirmations, make positive plans. In fact the old adage, "seek and you shall find", can definitely be used in your quest to give yourself a positive 'boost'.

9). At the end of each day, it is important that you go to bed with as little worry and negativity as possible. In bed, read inspiring and motivational material, listen to relaxing music that makes you feel good about yourself or listen to positive and inspiring CDs or downloads. You can also practice visualization techniques before falling asleep to help you *see* what your goals are and how you will accomplish them. Remember, you have to *see it to be it*!

10). Above all else, learn to *love yourself*. After all, once you love yourself you become more accepting and balanced as a person, and you can truly love other people in your life. You won't be needy or dependent, nor will you have any other negative emotions that leave you feeling debilitated. As a result, you will genuinely feel happier and more positive about everyone and everything in your life, and in particular, about *yourself*!

The benefits for you of implementing a 'positive thinking strategy' into your life are immense. When you work hard to dispel the negativity which you have allowed to dominate you, you will eventually see how you, and only you, have held yourself back in your life.

What are the benefits of thinking positively for you?

i). A change of attitude from negative to positive will help you to see more possibilities in your life, rather than the restrictions that you have been focusing on.

ii). A change of attitude from negative to positive will help you to feel more energetic, rather than feeling lethargic as you had done previously.

iii). A change of attitude from negative to positive will attract happier more positive people into your life, rather than surrounding yourself with people who always moan and complain about their existence.

iv). A change of attitude from negative to positive will make you healthier as you focus more on your dietary and exercise regimes, rather than feeling lethargic and listless all the time.

v). A change of attitude from negative to positive will create a happier and more joyous life for you, rather than being fearful, critical and worried all the time.

Of course, there are many other benefits to changing your attitude from negative to positive, these are just a few. To create new habits in your life, you need three to four weeks of practice. After this period of time, you can cut back a little in what you do, and create a *maintenance program* for yourself whereby, although you still practice positive thinking on a daily basis, you can be more balanced in your outlook as you know you have the power to control your negativity.

Note: It is important to understand your environment and everything that is involved in your life. Although a positive thinking programme is intended to create opportunities, possibilities and a better outlook for you, be careful that you don't create any *denial* in your life, whereby you refuse to see the inevitable sadness and pain that you may encounter at some point, or that you may see happening in the world on a daily basis. Positive thinking is about being constructive in your thinking and learning how to handle anything negative that may occur in your life. It is about creating a meaningful and productive life for yourself *no matter what external forces you may encounter.*

Positive thinking is about learning how to handle whatever life throws at you in the best and most optimal way for you. The key is understanding that difficult times, bad luck or adversity do not need to define or dominate your life. Denial creates hopelessness, inactivity and weakness, whereas positive thinking creates unbreakable strength, which leads to empowerment, which in turn leads to creating the best life possible for you.

"Weakness of attitude becomes weakness of character."

Albert Einstein

So far in this chapter, we have looked at a few tools and tips to help you think more positively in order to create a programme of positive thinking on a daily basis. We will now look at a few more general tips that you can incorporate into your lifestyle which, with use over time, will help you create a more positive outlook.

Be Grateful:

Gratitude plays an important role in leading to a happier life. Instead of focusing on what you *don't* have, focus on what you *do* have... and learn to be grateful for it. When you learn to understand and appreciate what you have, it creates a sense of achievement and inner peace in you, rather than a restless feeling of not having and needing something. Write down a list of ten things that you are grateful for in your life right now. Read them and appreciate them. Learn to give thanks for what you have been given, because sometimes in life, if we are not grateful, we may end up losing what we truly love or what we already have.

Don't Dwell On The Past:

It's easy to have regrets in your life and think about what you should have done and how you should have done it. Retrospect can be a great thing or a cruel thing depending on how you view it. If you are constantly 'beating yourself up' over your past, you will constantly be living in a world of negativity and regret. In fact, to a degree, there is no such thing as a 'mistake'. When you think about it, at any given time you make a decision, it is based on the information you have and the experience you have at *that* given time. Two, five or ten years later for example, new information or ideas may come to light to help you see things differently, but as time moves forwards, not backwards, it's important not to berate yourself for what you did or didn't do in the past. The past is over. The only thing that may keep it alive are your regrets … So make sure that you don't have any regrets!

Be Altruistic:

The power of giving should never be underestimated. Many a time, we are too absorbed in our own lives without due care or regard for other people. When we help others, it takes the focus away from us being self-absorbed and places our emphasis on what we can do for others.

You really do feel good about yourself if you can give something to others selflessly. You also understand much better the sentiment, "It is far better to give, than it is to receive"… When you feel that you are contributing to society in some way, you are left feeling contented, joyous and much more positive about yourself and about the world around you.

Surround Yourself With Positive People:

"Birds of a feather, flock together!" Sometimes, without realising, the people in our lives contribute to what we do and how we feel. Of course in all friendships for example, there will be natural ups and downs, where we support or receive support from our friends, but it's a good idea to analyze how some friends and family members leave you feeling. If people leave you feeling energized and good about yourself, then naturally, it's a good idea to spend more time with them. People who leave you feeling emotionally drained and are hard work to be around, should be avoided if possible, and if that's not possible, then see them sparingly. Other people's moods can be very infectious, so negative people can leave you feeling the way they do, and more relevantly to you, so can the mood of positive people.

Smile And Laugh More:

Just by smiling more, you actually feel happier... You trick your subconscious into thinking that you really are smiling and therefore your mind responds in a positive manner. So as hard as it may be if you're feeling sad and sorrowful about anything, force yourself to smile, and in a short time, you will start to feel better. Also, make it a mission of yours to watch more comedy on television, watch funny films, share funny stories and jokes with friends, in fact, if you are not naturally humorous, you will see a massive change in your demeanor in a short time, with a far more positive outlook. The benefits of laughter can include a boost of energy, a strengthened immune system, diminished pain, lowered stress levels and increased happiness and intimacy. Therefore, *laughter really is the best medicine*.

Redirect Your Thoughts:

This positive thinking technique is used a lot in counselling and therapy, and it can help you by controlling your thoughts whenever you start to feel anxious, sad and really down about something. Whenever you find yourself drifting into negative thoughts, you can become mindful of what you're thinking, resulting in you learning to redirect your thoughts to happier ones. You can start thinking of positive memories and images and you can start to give yourself positive feedback, so that you manage to keep the bad feelings and negative thoughts at bay.

Believe You Will Succeed:

Sometimes a general malaise in our way of thinking makes us doubt everything about ourselves. We forget all our achievements and successes and lose confidence in our abilities. When you start to believe that you will succeed, this belief will then help you create it as your successful reality. Always give yourself the benefit of the doubt and never be too hard on yourself. Having a deep-rooted belief in your abilities and knowing that you will succeed in fulfilling your goals, will create the positive thought patterns you are after.

Always Look For The Positives in Any Situation:

If you're a great believer in things happening for a reason, then you will already know that there are positives to be had where and when you least expect them. Sometimes, even the most negative things in our lives present us with opportunities that we wouldn't have been strong enough to pursue otherwise. Negative circumstances like losing your job or getting divorced can lead to you starting up your own business, travelling or re-educating yourself by taking up new courses. In essence, always bear in mind that if one door closes for you, MANY others may open for you, not just another one.

Positive thinking can be a part of your life if you choose it to be. There are many tips, tools and quotes that can inspire you, both in this book and others. Don't be a slave to your negative thoughts and feelings. If you want a more harmonious and positive life, though it may involve some hard work, it is definitely worth striving after.

CHAPTER SIX:

DEALING WITH THE NEGATIVES

"People too weak to follow their own goals will always find a way to discourage yours."

Anonymous

As you now begin to move forwards in your life – you are mastering positive thinking, you are feeling more empowered, you are going for your goals and you are facing your fears – you will start to encounter another more unexpected problem. The people closest to you in your life will lose *their* perspective of you. They are all used to you being and behaving in a certain way, and now, with your pattern of interaction being broken for good, you may experience confusion, upset and even negativity directed towards you.

Your perceptions up to now have been about dealing with your own demons and what you need to do to overcome them. When you start to change, you realise that your environment does also. In fact, a large part of counselling and therapy is also geared towards helping you cope not just with the changes in *you,* but also in the changes of others and *their* reactions to you.

Never lose sight of *your* goal. Always bear in mind that for you to grow as a person and become who you want and need to be, you *must have strong and motivated people in your life who inspire you.* Remember, if you want to move from being

Destructive to being Empowered you may need to make some serious changes in your life. So what signs do you need to look for to help you make the necessary changes?

Ask yourself the following questions:

- "Are the people in my life happy for me as I continue to grow, or would they prefer me to remain as I am?"

- "Do I feel good about myself when I am around these people, or does their negativity drag me down and leave me feeling drained?"

- "Do the people in my life support my changes, or are they being critical of me (again)?"

- "Are the people in my life appreciative of me and my changes, or do they take advantage of me and take me for granted?"

Your answers to the above questions should be a major indicator to how the people in your life are treating you, and in turn, how you may be treating yourself. Maybe rather inadvertently, you have been a part of the 'Negativity Club', and it's not until you are thinking in a different way that you realize this. The key to understanding this lies in *awareness* of what has been happening and what is continuing to happen with the people around you. When you start to understand your immediate environment and become aware of what is going on, you start to take the necessary measures to address the situation.

What is the outcome?

Once you have worked out the people around you, you will naturally want to avoid the negative and depressing ones. As you begin to take control of your life and emotions, the last thing you want to encounter is anything that will hold you back as you move forwards. Think of yourself as a ship sailing towards new waters, negative people are like anchors trying to hold you back and hold you down, keeping you rooted to where *they* want you to be. As difficult as it may be, sometimes you have to break away and venture to where *you* need to be in your life. As you become more discerning of everyone, you will notice that being positive and being negative have an 'energy' attached to them, and you will naturally find yourself being drawn to the positive energy in people. A good way to understand this is by knowing that the people in your life are a good indicator of where you are operating on an emotional level at that particular time. Being attracted to negative people actually says a lot about *you*, as does being attracted to positive people. Like is attracted to like. As you become more and more positive, you will both consciously and subconsciously seek out people similar to yourself.

In counselling and therapy, a common question that arises is:

"Should I just leave behind my old friends? As I won't have many friends left otherwise …"

In an ideal world, your new found energy and positivity should hopefully inspire and awaken your friends into being proactive and chasing after their dreams and goals. Together you could achieve a lot by supporting each other … and even if that happens, you shouldn't ignore the possibility of looking for new friends and new role-models to expand your support system.

Your new found support system should make you feel good about yourself, provide you with inspiration, help you when you need it and above all should be positive to your needs and aspirations.

What about old friends who aren't so supportive?

Depending on their level of negativity, you really do have to evaluate the friendship and work out if there are any benefits for you in maintaining it. If your friends sound like this:

- "That's brave of you, I would never do it ... you are bound to fail ..."

- "There's too much competition out there, I can't see you being successful ..."

- "Your relationship is bound to break down. I don't like the look of him/her ..."

- "That's too risky, if I were you, I wouldn't do it ..."

- "That course looks like it is too difficult, maybe you should just leave it ..."

- "Being positive *sounds* good, but how realistic do you think it is for you ..."

If any of the above sentences hit a chord with you, then maybe it's time to re-evaluate the people who keep feeding you with *their* negativity. Remember, like is attracted to like, at some point, you may not want them in your life anyway. As hard as it may be, some friendships don't last the test of time; you can't help it if you have outgrown them. Sometimes we have to 'leave a club that doesn't represent our ideals anymore, and join a new one that does'. Cancel your subscription to the 'Negativity Club' and join one that represents your new found beliefs and ideals. Your old friends will either be forced to re-evaluate their own beliefs or they will just move on to other people who are similar to them - negative!

We looked at role models earlier, and when you are looking to deal with the negatives in your life, a good way to do this is by finding inspiration from people who are *further on the path in their journey*. There's nothing wrong in finding a good mentor for you who can enlighten you in many aspects of your life and teach you things that you don't know. We are never too old to learn new things, or adapt to our environment, or to change to a more optimal way of being ... And there is nothing better than to receive a helping hand along the way. Once you have created a beneficial support group for yourself, your thoughts will naturally become more open and receptive to a better way of thinking. Don't remain too focused on your old friends. They will either drift away further into their negativity, or it could be the wake-up call they have been waiting for, and they may even follow in your footsteps.

How do you start?

We are lucky, because in this age of technology, we can use social media to get in touch with people we admire or we can get inspiration from the many positive role models that are available to us. It's important to make the effort. Try to do something that will get you in touch with, or enable you to be exposed to positive people and positive experiences. With social media and technology being the way it is, it is easy to find who and what you're looking for; there are always groups, and like-minded people on the internet you could be involved with. You could also meet new and interesting people in courses, self-improvement classes, presentations or seminars, just make the effort to reach out to people and you might connect with people on the level you are looking for. It's important to create that support group in your life and in reality, it could be a mix of real and virtual friends - people from all over the world you can interact with on a daily basis even.

What if your partner is the negative one?

All relationships have a 'balance and dynamic' that define them. When any of the parameters are shifted, it is only natural for a partner to feel uneasy about what is happening. If you decide that you need to lose weight, or you need to take a course, or you need a new job, or you need a new way of thinking, then your partner will invariably question the changes taking place and will also question the new balance/ dynamic of the relationship. After all, you may no longer be the person that he/she fell in love with. Bear in mind that you both may need some time to adjust to the changes that could occur in your relationship.

Let us look at some examples:

Sarah

Sarah is an attractive woman who always makes an effort when getting dressed and putting on her make-up. Looking at her now, you would never have guessed that just a couple of years earlier, she was very unhealthy. She was obese and at the same time she smoked twenty cigarettes a day. She was told by her doctor that she needed to lose weight and give up smoking, otherwise her health would seriously be compromised. She had two children, one child when she was eighteen from a violent ex-boyfriend, and another child from a relationship years later. She was now involved with a partner who seemed happy at how she was before and saw no issues with her weight or her smoking. The problems for him started when she lost a lot of weight, stopped smoking and got herself a job. The relationship went through lots of ups and downs before she finally gave him an ultimatum to accept her as she now was or move on from her life. After he had spent a long time subtly trying to undermine her by accusing her of flirting, trying to fatten her up with unhealthy food, sleeping in another room and trying to knock her newly gained confidence at every opportunity, he finally realized that it was *him* who had the problem and not her. He was actually very insecure deep down, and was worried about all the attention that Sarah was now getting, especially from men. Being from a small town, he found it very difficult to hear from everyone about how attractive she now was, and about all the compliments she was now getting. Eventually, after he confronted his issues, he was able to be more of a supportive partner for Sarah, rather than a critical partner who was scared deep down of losing her.

Lauren

Lauren had always been nervous and socially awkward growing up. She had many emotional problems which were brought on by her parents' unstable marriage and her being involved with the 'wrong types'. After her parents eventually split, she went off the rails for a while, before eventually settling down with someone from the town she came from. Over the years, her fears developed into social phobias and she found it very difficult to communicate with people, choosing to stay at home rather than going out and facing her fears. Her partner seemed very supportive of her and was happy to do everything for her as she chose to stay at home. Lauren sought the counselling and therapy she needed to overcome her issues, and eventually, she blossomed into a woman who went out, met friends, engaged with people, went shopping and did many other things for herself. She had totally transformed her life.

One day it dawned on her that her partner had been trying to sabotage her life. He had been trying to constantly fill her head with fears. He remained very aloof every time she tried to share positive stories with him and he kept trying to put her down at every opportunity. She realised that he was feeling very threatened by her newly found independence and freedom. Whereas before, her limitations meant that her life was very restricted, for him it meant he never had to worry about where she was, what she was doing and who she was with, and in reality this was a very secure relationship for him. He now didn't feel as needed as he had done previously. After some time, Lauren and her partner managed to discuss and work through all the difficulties and new challenges that her change had produced in the relationship. Her partner gradually came to terms with the new dynamics in the relationship and worked hard at dealing with his own issues, and ironically, he ended up receiving a lot of support and help from her. Again, the choice for him was, change or lose her. He chose to change.

In the above examples both Sarah's and Lauren's partners, with some difficulty at first, eventually understood their own insecurities and managed to work through their own problems, and as a result, it benefited both them and the relationship. Not all outcomes are as positive though. Here are a couple more examples, but with totally different outcomes:

Michael

Michael spent his life being fairly successful in various jobs, but the underlying motivating factor for him had always been safety and security. He was a good provider to his children from a previous relationship, but being in his forties now, Michael felt there had to be more to his life than just mundane office jobs and being a good provider. He was now married to his second wife and they also had a child together, whom he took good care of. Whilst Michael was looking for new opportunities, two possibilities arose which he decided he would take a risk and go after. He broached the subject with his wife, but after her initial enthusiasm, she became very unsupportive and struggled to deal with the change in Michael's ambition. He found a house that needed renovating and at the same time, also saw a small 'Bed and Breakfast' establishment that was up for sale. He planned to renovate the house and rent it out, and with the Bed and Breakfast property, he planned to relocate there with his wife and child, whilst also providing a place to stay and breakfast for paying customers. He managed to get the necessary capital for his projects, but despite this, his wife continued with her resistance and protests to his projected plans. Despite daily battles and arguments, Michael decided to go ahead with his plans.

Initially his wife followed him, but she continued to be unsupportive and resentful of his newly found ambition and risk-taking motivators. Not long after the move, the relationship disintegrated and Michael and his wife divorced. She continues to see him as being selfish and uncaring, because she felt her financial security had been compromised, and deep down she didn't have too much confidence in his ability to make a success of everything. After the divorce, despite it being very difficult financially for Michael, he remained optimistic and satisfied that he followed his dreams and goals until fruition. He is now looking for a partner who will help him grow as a man, and whom he plans to encourage to grow in return. His ex-wife is still single and bitter about the whole experience …

Tara

Tara came from a troubled background. Her parents were immigrants to Britain and Tara was only five years old when they moved to this country. During her childhood and adolescent years, Tara was fairly disruptive and didn't attend school as often as she should have. Her home life was very unstable, and Tara often stayed with friends and family rather than with her parents who constantly argued and rarely provided her with the care and nurture she needed. At the age of seventeen, she met someone and moved in to live with him and his family. Although they were very nice people, Tara felt very restless, as she knew deep down she hadn't achieved what she should have academically. She was a hard working girl and decided to go back to college. Her partner also worked hard and they eventually left the family home and set up a home together. Whilst Tara studied, everything seemed to be fine. Her partner, who was a builder, happily provided for their home and Tara worked part-time as well as continuing with her studies. Finally when Tara finished her studies and received her diploma, she felt very proud of herself as she knew she would be able to work in an environment she could only have dreamed of a few years earlier. Her partner wasn't as pleased unfortunately. The dynamic of their relationship had changed forever. He saw himself as 'just a builder', while her world had now expanded with huge possibilities for her.

He started to become more and more critical of her and put her down at every opportunity he could. She eventually got a very good job in the financial sector, while for him, as he struggled to deal with her success, he began staying out later and later, and drinking more and more. Inevitably, the relationship reached its natural conclusion, and after the split, Tara got together with a new partner whom she had met previously in college. She has never regretted going back to college, splitting up from her ex-partner and finding a new person to share her life with (they are now married with a child and live in a fairly nice part of town).

Of course your relationship or marriage is never something that you should be taking lightly, and if possible, you should always strive to improve and grow *together with your partner.* However, if you have a burning desire to achieve something, then it is almost impossible for you to just sit back and ignore it. If you feel that you are 'stagnating' and not being allowed to grow in your relationship, you may end up being resentful and harboring negativity towards your partner on a subconscious level anyway. Ultimately, your relationship may become too strained, and you could be heading for a breakdown of sorts.

A good rule to follow is:

BELIEVE THAT YOUR PARTNER WANTS THE BEST FOR YOU AND YOUR RELATIONSHIP AND THAT ANY

POSITIVE CHANGE IN YOU WILL ALSO RESULT IN A
POSITIVE CHANGE FOR THE RELATIONSHIP.

Logically thinking, your partner should want the best for you
and for you to find new energy and power because it will
surely re-invigorate your relationship, and ultimately benefit
the both of you.

Our partners should be happy and supportive of us, as we
should be of them. If your relationship has any elements of
neediness, helplessness and weakness, then you really have to
ask yourself if this is the type of relationship you really want
to be involved in. Is this what you envisaged for yourself
when you thought of being in a relationship?

It's not only our partners who can create problems for us as
we move towards our goals, our children can become difficult
and needy as they sense the change in us, our parents may be
judgmental and critical of anything that results in change. The
reason for all this is that our children and parents have become
accustomed to interacting with us and relating to us in a
certain way… And now, we are shifting the goal-posts for
them, they don't quite know what to make of it.

Typical responses are:

*- Children will try to manipulate you at every opportunity or
even make you feel guilty about what you are doing or
planning to do.*

*- Parents with their subtle put-downs and reminders of your
past failings, in an effort to undermine what you are now
working towards and trying to achieve.*

Sometimes parents really aren't aware of their put-downs and
words which knock your self-confidence and belief in
yourself. It usually starts when you're young and can continue
throughout your life. Even when you point out what they are
doing, they are often the *masters of denial,* and don't admit to

143

their foibles and negativity. If you're lucky, they may change over time, but if not, then you have to develop many self-defense mechanisms to cope with their idiosyncrasies.

If you are lucky, you may have a fully functional, totally supportive family behind you, but that is usually not the case. With the love of a family usually comes a great deal of possessiveness and manipulation, in fact, in any other relationship, it could be construed as extremely harmful if not damaging. But with family, we usually accept what is directed towards us, after all, as is usually said, 'you can't choose your family...' We tend to accept any negativity and crazy behaviour as being 'normal'. It is very difficult at times trying to balance a family and keep everyone happy, but developing techniques to create 'win-win' outcomes is vital.

What you have to be extremely careful of, is that you don't become ultra-defensive of yourself and what you are pursuing. This may result in you lashing out at your nearest and dearest every time you perceive their negativity as a personal attack or criticism of you. Be careful you don't create what I call the *'Personality Swing Syndrome'*. As you strive to create assertiveness for your new actions and behaviour, you may end up going from Passivity to Aggression, before you settle in the Healthy Assertiveness area of behaviour. When you go from Passivity to Aggression you usually swing from one extreme to the other. So from saying nothing, you usually say things like:

- "How the hell would you know?"

- "What's it got to do with you anyway!"

- "I'm going to do whatever makes me happy, so get used to it!"

- "I've stopped caring about what you think, remember it's MY life!"

- "If you've got a problem with it, you know what you can do!"

Below you can see how the **Personality Swing Syndrome** works:

STARTING BEHAVIOR	GOAL	EXTREME BEHAVIOR

INAPPROPRIATE	APPROPRIATE	INAPPROPRIATE
Passivity	Healthy Assertiveness	Aggression

$\underline{1}$

$>$ $<$

$\underline{2}$

 $>$ $<$

$\underline{3}$

   $>$ $<$

$\underline{4}$

    $>$ $<$

$\underline{5}$

      $>$ $<$

$\underline{6}$

$><$

$\underline{7}$

The diagram shows how our behaviour starts as extreme Passivity (Inappropriate), then it can swing over to extreme Aggression (Inappropriate), and as we go through different levels, our behavior may continue to swing from one side to the other. As we go down further through different levels of development, our swings aren't as extreme until we finally reach our desired point (6/7) of Healthy Assertiveness (Appropriate) with no more swings of varying degrees to inappropriate behaviors of Passivity or Aggression.

As you go through the process of change, it is understandable that the new behaviors you are trying to incorporate into your life are not yet a part of you. As a result, you become totally defensive and overly aggressive as a balance to the passivity which is still a part of you, but which you are fighting against. These behavioral extremes to Aggression occur because you are trying to hang onto your new behaviour for dear life, and the fear that you have relates to you not wanting to go back to being Passive again. However, every so often, you will naturally swing back to your 'comfort zone' of Passivity. As a result of this, your behavior will swing back and forth from being Passive to being Aggressive until Healthy Assertiveness becomes a part of your behavioral pattern. In reality, it means that your behavior swings from being inappropriate many times before it settles into the appropriate range, and it is in this range that we become comfortable expressing our desires and needs and doing what we want to do. Please be aware that in the beginning, these behavior swings really are a reality which will cause a lot of angst for you and your loved ones until your behavior becomes more healthy and appropriate.

Without realising, we go through many fearful new behavioral changes throughout our lives. Many things happen to us along the way and as a result we subconsciously adapt our behavioral patterns to the new environments we may find ourselves in. These changes cause difficulty and upheaval for us until we learn to behave in a new way.

In fact, *Awareness* is the key here. Develop the *Mindset* that as you continue to grow, you are going to get resistance from other people in your life. That is a *fact*. Partners, friends, parents, children, you name it, someone will 'rock the boat' for you at some point. Be one step ahead, understand that their observations and criticisms are because they are defending *their* security in how they interact with you.

There may also be positive support for you from some people, not just resistance. Some friends and family may be helpful and nurturing, and it's important for you to acknowledge their support. By appreciating the encouragement from others in your life, it will reinforce the reactions that you are seeking from people, and help you focus on the positives that you will also find, rather than focusing on any negativity from people.

Awareness of the Personality Swing Syndrome will help you to overcome some of your behavioral swings, and also help you to deal with any criticism more appropriately. As mentioned earlier, when dealing with negative feedback, it is important to look for 'win-win' outcomes and scenarios. It really means that you have to constantly be aware of creating a situation where *everyone wins and is left satisfied with the outcome*. Below you will find a few examples of how you would start a 'win-win' discussion:

Wife: "Just look at yourself. You've become so self-centered and egotistical since you've started that job. Do you really think you're so special now?"

Lose-Lose Response: "That's a bit rich coming from you! How can *you* call *me* selfish? I've been supportive of everything you've done over the years, now it's *my* turn, so back off a little!"

Win-Win Response: "I know I'm not around as much as I used to be, and while you may construe that as being selfish, I really need to do this for my own growth and I would be extremely grateful for your support. If I don't follow my dreams and goals now, I will end up being angry and resentful towards myself and towards you anyway. I know it's only natural for you to be feeling left out and neglected, but I am honestly not being selfish here. I do love you and will do anything to help improve the situation for you."

Parent: "How many times have you now tried? You know it's extremely difficult, and you will never succeed at it. You may as well give up!"

Lose-Lose Response: "Just leave me alone and mind your own business! As always I'll do as I please thank you very much!"

Win-Win Response: "Actually I have a lot of belief and faith in myself, and I can deal with anything that comes my way. I appreciate your concern, but how about having a little more faith in me … That would really benefit me and I would be very appreciative also …"

Friend: "I've noticed that all your relationships go badly wrong. I've been thinking … There must be something wrong with you!"

Lose-Lose Response: "Look who's talking. 'Pot calling the kettle black' springs to mind! It's not as if *you're* such a great relationship expert yourself. You have had more disasters than I have, so sort *yourself* out first!"

Win-Win Response: "I know things haven't always worked out the way I would have hoped, but I am sure there is someone out there for me. I think *together* we can draw on our experiences and help each other to move forwards and find someone who is suitable for us. Maybe if we draw up a check-list together, that might help us find more suitable relationships …"

Children: "You don't love us as much as you used to and you don't care as much for us either. You're never at home anymore …"

Lose-Lose Response: "The problem with you kids today is that you are so self-centered. You should be more grateful for all the toys and games we have bought you and for all the running around we do after you. For once I'm doing something for myself and just listen to you, moaning and groaning and being totally un-appreciative as ever!"

Win-Win Response: "I can understand that you are unhappy because things feel a little different for you … I know you are used to how everything was before, but I need to do this course, and I'm sure that for a few hours a week, you can both cope without me. This course is important for me, so show me the same respect that I show you when you go to school and then have homework to do …"

What may help you to maintain control of yourself at all times is practicing 'Grounding/Centering Techniques'. These may include meditation, relaxation, using positive self-talk, yoga, pilates, etc., in fact any technique that helps you zone into a more peaceful place. Whenever you feel you are swinging from one extreme to another, these techniques can help to bring you back 'to the center' - a place of balance and harmony.

Look at it as a way of keeping you stable, grounded and maintaining your inner peace to keep you from losing control of a situation (or yourself!) or from getting too carried away. Grounding and Centering involves visualization and meditation to help you focus on the present and be more aware of your surroundings. Whenever you feel nervous, worried or stressed even, you can use these techniques to help you 'live in the moment'.

Here are some techniques to help you:

1). Start ~ Sit in a chair with your feet on the ground:

Choose a nice, quiet place without disturbances to help you zone in to a relaxing mindset.

2). Focus on your breathing:

Clench and tighten your stomach muscles and breathe up high in your chest. This type of 'chest breathing' is not deep breathing and is often an unconscious reaction to stress, anxiety or panic.

3). Relax:

Now unclench your stomach muscles and deep breathe down into your stomach. Try to imagine the air flowing down into your toes. To help you practice, put your hand on your stomach and breathe so that your stomach then pushes your hand out as you inhale, and then your hand comes back in as you exhale. Practice deep breathing until it becomes easy and natural for you.

4). Close your eyes:

Imagine your breath pushing down into the base of your spine and through your feet. If you feel any tension or fear, imagine that you are breathing out any negativity through your feet and out of your body. Continue to breathe deeply and imagine any negative emotion being released from your body.

5). Imagine:

Use your imagination and imagine your feet also drawing up energy and heat from the ground, then feel that energy and heat passing back up into your body.

6). Feel the heat:

Imagine that heat flowing through your body, up through your spine, into your lungs and heart, and anywhere else that needs extra energy. As you feel that heat and energy flowing through you, raise and open up your posture and re-focus on your breathing.

7). Direct the energy up:

Feel the energy through your arms and into your hands, through your neck and up to the top of your head. Visualize the energy passing out of you and upwards, then back around you like a protective shield. Feel that energy enveloping your body both internally and externally.

8). More energy and heat:

Continue your deep breathing; feel the heat and energy re-entering your body and draw it back into your heart, stomach and all your extremities.

9). Open your eyes:

Slowly feel the relaxation in your body, and after a few moments, feel the energy revitalizing you and leaving you feeling more refreshed and attentive.

10). Feel the ground under you:

Focus on your feet and your connection to the floor. Walk around a little and feel the ground under you. If at all possible, do this exercise outside and walk around bare-footed to feel a stronger connection with the ground and earth.

11). Stretch:

Stretch your arms out to your side as you focus straight ahead of you. Move and wiggle your fingers and thumbs. Now walk slowly, keeping your feet grounded and breathing deeply. Activate your peripheral vision, so you feel aware of what is going on around you.

12). Zone back to reality:

As you become aware of your surroundings again, focus on your breathing and your feelings of being grounded and centered. How would you describe this state of being? If you can use images, touch or phrases to describe it, then you can create an 'Anchor' (Anchor = a fixed psychological connection/point) to help you get grounded quickly in any future situation.

Techniques like the one above will help you to remain calm and have better control of yourself when you are faced with negativity of any kind - both internally and externally.

One major factor why we act with such hostility when others don't support us is because of our deep-rooted *need for approval.* You may or may not be aware of this, but this child-like need of ours, will also create child-like responses from us. Another reason for this hostility is *Guilt*; this masks our anger at ourselves and others for our inability to break unhealthy ties with loved ones. The Aggression part of the Personality Swing Syndrome comes from this unhealthy attachment that we have.

Becoming clearer and more concise with an adult-like way of behaviour in your efforts to grow, means that the people in your life can say anything they want to, and it won't have any adverse effect on you. In many ways, your need to please others shows what you still need to work on, that is; *learning to let go emotionally of your child-like role, and stepping into your role of an adult.* As difficult as this may be, you have to break these child-like relationships which will perpetuate your negative behaviors and substitute them with more adult-like ones which will create a greater element of responsibility. What you will learn, is that paradoxically, *the less you strive to attain someone's approval, the more approval you will receive from them.*

You have to redefine your relationships, and the best way to do that, is to look at all your personal relationships as a 'gauge' to work out where you are, and where you need to be. You can learn to let go of your inappropriate reactions and develop a more responsible way of behaving. For example, every time someone close to you makes you angry, it is better to look at them as your 'mirrors' so they can help you see yourself as you truly are and also help you to see what you need to work on with regards to your own personal growth.

Sometimes though, the people closest to you really do behave in a destructive manner towards you. What should you then do if that's the case?

* Jane had an up and down relationship with her parents for many years. Especially with her father. And after her parents divorced, Jane struggled to deal with her father's erratic behaviour and put downs. She tried to maintain a civil relationship with him for years. She visited him and called him like a dutiful daughter should, but eventually the put downs became too much for her. One day, after years of trying, Jane realised her father was never going to change, so she decided enough was enough, and she told him how she felt in no uncertain terms:

"For many years now I have put up with all your insults and constant criticism. I have overlooked things many times, which in retrospect maybe I shouldn't have. I feel that by me continuing to ignore your behaviour, I have *enabled* you to behave towards me the way that you have done. I have forgiven you over and over again and looked to make a fresh start every time, but each time I do, you hurt me by doing or saying something stupid again. I don't have the energy to keep doing this, and as much as it pains me, I have to cut you out of my life until maybe one day in the future when you can see the error of your ways and treat me with the level of respect that I feel I deserve …"

As a result, Jane has stayed away from her father for many years. As difficult as it has been, it was something she felt she needed to do in order to build up her levels of self-confidence and inner strength again. Sometimes, saying goodbye to a parent and an old relationship usually requires an element of 'grieving', because as one thing ends, time will be needed before another thing (new relationship) can begin. We mourn in a sense the 'end of an era', and no matter how satisfying a new beginning will be, we still go through the 'Grieving Process'- Denial, Anger, Bargaining, Depression/Grief and eventually Acceptance.

For Jane, she is far more optimistic when she thinks of her father now, and although she is resigned when she thinks of his behaviour in the past, she hopes that one day she will re-connect with her father and he will have seen the error of his ways.

Ironically for Jane, the only way she has a chance of gaining her father's respect is by *teaching* him how to respect her on her terms. With her higher levels of confidence and inner strength, her father will know on some level that she can happily cope without him. Ultimately, this will be the way she will gain his respect in the future: *by him knowing she has the capability and strength to cope without him in her life.*

Always consciously have the thought that *you are your own best friend in this world!* Never criticize yourself and never put yourself down. Eventually you will work out where you need to be in your life and what you need to do to get there. To gain the respect of others, firstly *you have to respect yourself,* and secondly, *you have to give them something to respect.* If you lose people along the way, then so be it, because your new inner strength and self-confidence will allow you to break unhealthy relationships, and in time, establish new and healthier ones.

"You are essentially who you create yourself to be and all that occurs in your life is the result of your own decision making."

Stephen Richards

CHAPTER SEVEN:

DECISION MAKING

"You can suffer the pain of change, or suffer remaining the way you are."

Joyce Meyer

One of the biggest problems we encounter when we have clouded thought processes and emotional difficulties, relates to our *decision making* processes. This is because our minds are in a constant *battle* between intuition and logic for every decision we face. This conflict plays out in every aspect of our lives, from what we believe, to who we fall in love with, from what we eat, to what we decide to do, and most powerfully of all, in all our decisions relating to money. Due to this constant battle between logic and intuition, when we make random errors of judgement, they may not always be 'random errors', in fact, they are based on certain biases we have already created.

Here are a couple of common indecision type problems:

* Patrick: "I have so many thoughts going around and around in my mind, that I really struggle when it comes to making decisions. Sometimes I feel as though I am stuck between a rock and a hard place and I end up procrastinating and doing nothing just to avoid making a decision. In fact, I have been like this throughout my life. I just can't decide anything."

* Lucy: "I sometimes feel as though I am really missing out in life. I always find it difficult to work out what I truly want. Often times, I avoid having to decide things, just so I don't have to think about it, or I just agree to everything, so that it becomes a lot easier for me … though in reality it doesn't, it just complicates matters even more. I wish I could just decide what was best for me."

The ironic thing in the above two examples, is that by choosing not to deal with their issues and confront their inability to make a decision, they actually *are* making a decision. The decision to do NOTHING! The real fear when it comes to struggling to make decisions is that deep in our psyche, we believe ALL decisions to be either right or wrong. In our minds we believe that making the wrong decision may equate to losing something or depriving ourselves of something. That something could be status, or respect, or money, or lovers, or friends, or whatever else we may deem as being lost if we don't make the *right* decision. Therefore, we tend to be naturally careful.

Added to this is our desire to be the best or to be perfect in what we do. There are many people out there who constantly strive for perfection. Are you one of them? If you are, then this need to be 'perfect' all the time can hide an underlying desire to *control* outcomes and events in your life. Perfectionism is more about maintaining constant and total control and correlates to a fear of change or attempting something new, because if you do, you may not be able to control the outcome. The irony here is that in life, we learn a lot by making "mistakes".

If fear is holding you back in your life and manifesting itself as perfectionism, needing to be in control or being overly analytical, then you have to understand that you can control these thoughts and create scenarios you desire by *changing the way you think*. Your goal in reality is to make it possible never to make a wrong decision or never to make a "mistake" again.

If you could do this then you would never procrastinate in your life and you would be proactive at every opportunity, wouldn't you?!

How is this possible?

Up until now in your life, you have been programed to follow a 'No-Win Outcome' for every choice you have had to make. When faced with a decision, maybe it has left you feeling paralyzed, or worried, or even being obsessed about what you should do. For example:

- "What if I do this and that happens …?"

- "Should I go for this or should I go for that …?"

- "What if it goes all horribly wrong for me …?"

- "What if …?"

The "What if" scenarios run over and over in your mind creating doubt, confusion and ultimately procrastination. You either end up trying to predict the future, or you end up trying to control external forces. Either way, whatever you are thinking, it is not possible. Also, your negative thought processes usually take over, and dominate your thinking processes: whatever you choose is "risky or won't work out anyway"! You run over certain scenarios again and again trying to figure out the best course of action, with the least possible damaging returns.

This is what a No-Win scenario would look like:

NO-WIN OUTCOME

RIGHT?	< DECISION >	WRONG?
WRONG?	POINT	RIGHT?

When you are at your decision making point, you are torn between what you should do and which direction you should take. Maybe if you decide something, it could be right (or wrong), but if you choose something else, it could be wrong (or right). In the above scenario, you can see, it will always end-up as a No-Win Outcome for you. Whatever decision you have made, you will constantly re-assess the situation, hoping you didn't make a mistake. If you do this constantly, it can end-up being very debilitating, as you always search for alternatives …

- "Maybe I should have done this instead …"

- "If only I had chosen to do that …"

You may gain temporary respite if the decision you have made works out well for you, but even then, you may be worried that in the future it will backfire on you and turn out as badly as you had envisaged it would. Also, this whole process will start up all over again the *next* time you have a decision to make. So it will be a constant mental battle for you as you worry and deliberate over what to do. This process will happen again and again with every decision that needs to be made.

However, there is another way for you, a better way to make decisions.

The Win-Win Outcome.

Go back to your Decision Point again and imagine now that you have two choices, 'Choice A' and 'Choice B'. Imagine in your mind that *both these choices are right!* Each choice has nothing but *rewards* along the way for you.

So what are these *rewards* you are no doubt asking?

Think of them as life opportunities to learn and develop, to find out your limits and who you really are, to work out what you would like to do and who you would like to become, and think of these rewards as gaining new experiences in your life. See them as 'life lessons' that money can't buy.

So what does the Win-Win outcome look like?

WIN-WIN OUTCOME

CHOICE A   <   **DECISION**   >   **CHOICE B**
RIGHT!   (Rewards)   **POINT**   (Rewards)   **RIGHT!**

In the Win-Win model above, whatever choice you make is the right one with many opportunities, possibilities and rewards along the way. This will always result in a 'Win-Win' situation for you *whatever you choose and whatever the outcome!*

So how is this possible?

Imagine you are faced with making a major life-changing decision, such as moving home, starting up your own business, changing jobs or splitting up with a partner. All of these scenarios can be difficult, challenging and angst ridden. What you may also find is that your negative thoughts and negative voices whirl around in your mind creating no-win outcomes for you. For example, if we look at changing jobs, your negative inner voice may sound something like this:

* Javier: "What should I do? I have no idea which course of action to take. What if the new job is too difficult with too much responsibility which I may struggle, to handle. Then what? I may get fired. If I leave this job, I may be missing out on being promoted in the future. I do like it here when I think about it. I know what to do and my colleagues are all nice. I may regret leaving. Actually, what if I do get fired, then I will have nothing! Should I just focus on what will bring me more money? Oh I hate making decisions like this… I really don't know what to do. I could ruin *everything* if I make the wrong decision…"

You can see in the above example the never ending questioning and doubting that can take place. Also, these types of questions and doubts, as mentioned, are prevalent when you're looking to start up your own business, figuring out whether to end a relationship, whether to move home or not, or even making a choice between potential suitors! Whatever decisions you have to make can result in you ending up mentally exhausted and even exacerbating the situation as you flip from one possible outcome to another.

Looking at your situation from a Win-Win viewpoint will provide you with many more opportunities, *positives* and rewards. For example:

* Dougie: "This is a great opportunity for me one way or another. If I take this job offer, I will get to meet new people, work in an exciting new environment, experience a new way of doing things and broaden my work knowledge. Even if it doesn't work out the way I hope, I know I can cope, what with my work experience, confidence and self-belief, I have no doubts something else will turn up. I will then have to learn new skills like coping while I'm looking for a better job. Even if I stay here, I might ask for a promotion and a salary increase now that I know I have other possibilities, and if I do end up staying here, I can develop my contacts and connections in

this firm. Who knows what the future will bring, I could end up staying here and then get offered an even better job in the future anyway. It's all good, whatever I decide to do!"

When you think about it, the reality of a situation really is your perception of it. If you see it as bad, then it is, and if you see it as good, then likewise, it's good. If that is clear to you, then you should realise that whatever obstacle, challenge or decision comes your way, then how you *choose* to face it is paramount in how it is resolved. One way or another whatever fear, worry or difficulty you may have in your life, it will have to be faced, so the earlier you try to resolve it, with the correct mental approach, then the better the outcome will be.

It's vital that you trust and believe in yourself and that you know you can deal with/handle any situation or challenge that comes your way.

Always remember:

THE BELIEF AND KNOWLEDGE THAT YOU CAN HANDLE ANYTHING THAT LIFE THROWS AT YOU, IS THE KEY IN ALLOWING YOURSELF TO TAKE RISKS.

As difficult as it may be for you to move forwards in your life, always *have courage in your convictions*, because that way, you will feel more confident in whichever direction you wish to take. It can sometimes be daunting for you to work out what you want to do in your life, but an important tip to bear in mind is that paradoxically, finding out what you *don't like* is as valuable as finding out what you *do like*. Even if something doesn't work out for you the way you had hoped, you still gain something from the experience.

"FOR EVERYTHING THAT DOESN'T WORK OUT FOR ME, SOMETHING GOOD WILL COME FROM IT!"

Write that down somewhere and use it as a mantra every time you need motivation to push yourself forward from indecision or a troubling situation.

- If a relationship doesn't work out for you, you WILL move on to find someone better suited for you.

- If a job interview doesn't work out for you, you WILL move on to find an even better job.

- If working in a particular company doesn't work out for you, you WILL move on to a company that matches your ideology much better.

In fact, whatever you may view as 'not working out' for you, will lead on to something that is much better for you. Very few people are still in the first relationship, or first job, or first house, or first anything else for that matter, that they were *firstly* involved with. Remember: There is no such thing as a 'mistake' because at that particular point in your life, you chose something/someone for a reason which later, either didn't work out as planned or because you developed in another unforeseen direction. Therefore, always think of a situation or choice as something that will develop in its natural course of action. So why be afraid, fearful or worried? There are no 'wrongs' or 'mistakes'- *Everything will develop as it is meant to naturally!*

Any negative emotion or feeling you may attach to moving forwards in your life has an underlying fear, and that fear is a *lack of trust in yourself and your ability*. You have to look at every step of every decision you make as an opportunity to learn to trust yourself. Also understand that you will gain some benefit from *whatever* happens to you.

You need to comprehend the implications of your thinking. If you continually have a subconscious No-Win attitude in all your dealings, you will always be a victim. As your objective is to be more assertive, feel more empowered and rid yourself of fears and negativity, it is imperative that you see your life as full of No-Lose/Win-Win possibilities and opportunities. You need to challenge yourself and ask yourself why you continually believe that negative equals realistic and positive equals unrealistic. Your beliefs will always perpetuate your outcomes:

No-Win Beliefs = Fear, Pain and Procrastination

Win-Win Beliefs = Positivity, Optimism and Opportunity

We are all focused on and geared towards success in our lives, so it would be natural for you to struggle with a Win-Win concept when you relate it to a marriage break-up or a job loss for example. Accepting a Win-Win model into your way of thinking is critical because it will challenge your traditional beliefs about what opportunities and success equate to. For most people, the idea of success relates to money, power, material possessions and status. Understanding a Win-Win model requires a new way of accepting what success means. If you can equate success to having inner strength and belief in yourself, being able to cope with any external factors, and trusting you will overcome adversity, then that will boost your self-esteem and diminish your levels of fear. Surely that is what success is all about …

Whenever something ends, something new begins. That is inevitable. That is the *Law of Nature*. Days end and are followed by new days. Seasons end are followed by new seasons. Years end and are followed by new years. Life ends and is followed by new life. We cannot change the principals of how everything works. In your life you have no doubt seen relationships end, and new ones begin, jobs end which are then followed by new opportunities, friendships end only for new ones to begin. Every ending is an opportunity to start again and strengthen your inner-resolve and self-esteem as you reach out once again and overcome the hurdles and challenges you have previously faced.

We have all suffered some adversity in our lives: illness, the death of a loved one, losing friendships, divorce, losing a job, bankruptcy, etc. (Even if we haven't, at some point, unfortunately, we will have to face something that tests our resolve). If you have suffered extreme adversity, you know that you end up much stronger than before and this strength comes from knowing that *'security is not about having things, it's about handling things'*. Once you truly understand that you can handle anything, you have no fear, you know you can approach anything with a Win-Win guarantee.

It's important to be *aware* of your alternatives whenever you have troubling thoughts. (*Awareness is your ability to feel, to perceive or to be conscious of objects, events, or your sensory patterns). This is important because when you are aware of all your alternatives, you know there are no rights or wrongs and whatever course of action you take, it will always result in a Win-Win scenario for you. This awareness will also enable you to be in better control of your outcomes as they match your wishes and desires, and ultimately for you, this will all lead to a much greater sense of inner calm and inner peace.

For many people, there are underlying issues and emotional struggles that inhibit them in creating the life they want for themselves. Making any decision to move ahead is a paralyzing process, but the key here is to understand it is not fatal nor is it irreversible. Inertia can be overcome when you take the right steps in making major decisions.

AWARENESS > BETTER CONTROL > POSITIVE OUTCOMES > PEACE OF MIND

The Psychology of Making a Decision

In fact, our daily lives are really one long sequence of choices and decision making and every day we make between two thousand and ten thousand different decisions. We are continually deciding: what to do; what to eat; when to talk; when to listen; when to move; when to stay still; and so on. Psychologists have worked out that we all have two systems for making decisions; Fast (System 1) and Slow (System 2). Fast = Automatic and Effortless. This is our 'normal' state of being and is responsible for what we do, and how we respond to external stimuli. Slow = Deliberate, Logical and Rational. This is the part of us that is the 'voice in our head' that we looked at and touched upon earlier. System 1 is like a reflex, giving us instant answers to our environment and also to our opinions. System 2 provides us with 'reasons' for our instant decisions and opinions, and in reality, it is this system that steers us through life. Think of System 1 as being fast, intuitive and powerful; and System 2 as being clever, logical and overly slow. In fact, this is where "mistakes" may creep in for us- when we use the wrong system to make decisions. Note: System 1 is like our 'auto pilot', it thoughtlessly creates habits for us and after we make a decision, we make others to follow that original decision, as if that first decision was actually meaningful!

When we make an important decision, we don't in fact look at the decision to be made, what we do, is actually compare it to and use *other* decisions that we made in the past. It's as if we have convinced ourselves that those previous decisions were good; "Oh, I've made that decision before ..." Our minds then short-cut to the decision from before (maybe with some modifications) and relate it to the new decision that we are now making. This results in an 'Anchoring' effect, whereby the mind uses System 1 which is the quickest possible route to a decision, but it should really be using System 2. This results in us making "mistakes". (Remember, System 2 requires more thought, logic and rationality). It could also explain why people continually date the 'wrong types', choose the wrong friends, repeatedly make bad investments, etc., etc.

This means that we are prone to systematic "mistakes", which are called "Cognitive Biases". Another detrimental bias we have, is the "Present Bias Focus", which makes us choose to do and create unhealthy behaviour patterns such as, drinking, smoking, over eating, etc, and this is because we focus on the present and don't think too much about the future. In this example, our choices and decisions are based in the short term, and not beyond that.

Another common flaw when we make decisions is that we *get attached to things that we ourselves have created*. This again clouds our rationality and as a result, we don't make the correct decisions. It is very common in situations where we repeatedly give people chances, or continually put up with harmful or destructive behaviors from others, because we can't make the correct decisions for ourselves in those situations. It also results in us doggedly continuing with something, when in reality we should just give up on it.

Sometimes we choose to overlook certain maladaptive behaviors in others, because of something called the 'Halo Effect'. If we like a certain aspect of someone, then we associate *everything* connected to that person as being good. Our minds choose to overlook any flaws that person may have. (The same can be observed in the negative sense, whereby one negative trait of a person, then becomes the overriding total impression).

We have to continually be aware of our decisions because we may be pre-programmed to patterns of decision making. It could be said that there may be just a few ways to do the 'right thing', but many ways for us to do the 'wrong thing'. (What may be referred to as "wrong" and "mistakes" in the Psychology of Making a Decision, relates to doing things that affect you *adversely*, such as, continually succumbing to temptations, impulsive spending, choosing unhealthy habits, trusting the wrong people, not having respect for other people and their views, and so forth, otherwise everything else can be viewed as a *healthy* learning process).

A common mistake people make in terms of choices and decisions relates to them believing that other people are interested in them or that others overly pay attention to them ('Spotlight Effect'), when in reality they don't! This can cause the afflicted person to make bad judgments about themselves and their surroundings as a result.

Another area where decision making is important relates to money. Some psychology studies suggest that losses are twice as powerful psychologically as gains are. This means our natural tendency, choices and decisions are geared towards protecting what we have/ avoiding losses rather than acquiring gains (This is known as the *Loss Aversion Bias*).

The vital point to remember in decision making is that, by accepting your own fallibility, you will come to a better understanding of your own mind. Only then can you address what you need to and take the necessary steps that will help you move forwards and make better decisions for yourself.

Bearing all this in mind, what should you do to help you overcome your fears when it comes to making the necessary decisions that will help you move forwards in your life?

BEFORE MAKING A DECISION

1. *Focus On Your Win-Win Outcomes:*

Practice positive thinking techniques and push out any negative thoughts: focus *only* on what you can gain. Use positive mantras to help you focus, such as, "My world is full of opportunity for me, everything that happens to me is a chance for me to grow and learn from. Everything happens for a reason, whatever happens, I can't lose, I will get something from whichever direction I choose to take ..." Repeating these types of positive sentences will reinforce your belief that whatever the outcome, you *will be able to deal with it and handle it*.

2. *Work Out Your Alternatives*:

There are many avenues open to you where you can glean information from in your efforts to find the alternatives available to you. There are many mentors out there for you, people who can provide you with invaluable information that can help you, or professionals such as coaches and counsellors who can point you in the right direction. You may be surprised at how many people may be forthcoming with useful advice and tips. Whatever your plans, it's important you don't let any negativity affect your visions and goals. Remember, *information clarifies your intention to make it happen*. Intention is a powerful tool for you; it creates something that you want to happen in your life.

Also, in this day and age, finding out information is much easier than it has ever been. As well as books and other publications, the internet has become a god-send for the curious mind. You can look for and find out anything you want to, and it's all at your fingertips. There really is no excuse for you not to do your homework when it comes to gaining as much information as possible before making the best and most educated decision for yourself. (Social media again, is another modern tool to help you gain access to what you are looking for and find out things you need to know).

3. *Work Out Your Priorities:*

Give yourself the necessary time you need to work out what you truly want in your life. It's important to dig deep and do some soul searching, however painful it may be for you. Many times in our lives we are dutiful and look to please everyone else who is involved in our lives. It starts young: parents, teachers, friends, family, partners, husbands or wives, in fact we may spend most of our lives trying to satisfy the expectations of other people. When you are a *bona fide* people pleaser, it's always going to be difficult for you to work out your *own* needs and priorities.

You really do need to work out your goals, but also bear in mind that throughout your life, your circumstances will change, and so will your goals accordingly. Sometimes you may re-evaluate what your aims are and change them along the way. Five years ago you were a different person, as you will be five years from now, so when you think about it, over a ten year period your goals may well chop and change until you find out where you need to be heading. Think of it as a natural experimentation process until you find clarity in your own needs and priorities.

4. *Follow Your Instinct:*

Sometimes no matter how much information you have acquired and how much analysis you have done, it still comes down to you having to decide which course of action you need to take. It's important therefore to listen to your instincts, because your subconscious mind will continually send you *knowing* messages as to what you should do at whatever juncture you come to. Pay attention to and trust your instincts, because ultimately the best advice comes to you from *yourself...* after all, no one knows you like you do! As we looked at earlier, don't make hasty decisions which may not work out for you, instead listen to your logical and rational mind which drives your subconscious instincts.

In your life, you may have an idea or plan for yourself as to what you should be doing, and sometimes something unexpected pops up which leaves you questioning what you should do next:

* Maria had studied psychology and always saw herself as a therapist once she gained her diploma:

"For me, it was never a question of doing anything different, other than being a full-time therapist in my life. After I got my diploma, I started counselling clients and my goal was always to start up my own private practice. Then a good friend of mine suggested I work with her on a new health concept she had started. My gut instinct was to join my friend and venture into a totally new direction. My logical mind was telling me not to deviate from my original plans, but my subconscious mind kept telling me to override those thoughts and take some risks. I am so glad I followed my intuition and instincts. Within a few months of joining my friend, I was made a partner and the business took off and became very successful. Sometimes you are in the right place at the right time, but even so, you *still* need to make a decision and follow your instincts. For me, it worked out extremely well, even if it hadn't, I would have worked as a therapist and been *just as happy* ..."

For Maria, as she alluded to, she proved the point that there are no right or wrong decisions, just different ones, and the path to success can take unexpected turns along the way. Trusting in your instincts can mean following your heart, or your gut feelings over something, but however you look at it, it is not necessarily a scientific process, more one of a *feeling* that you can't always put your finger on. Sometimes all the evidence may point in one direction, yet for whatever reason, for *you* it doesn't feel quite right, therefore you need to do what your instincts tell you; and your instincts are an innate part of your deeper understanding of who you are. (Note: Your Natural Instincts should *not be confused* with the Biases that you have created for yourself, and which you hastily may revert to when it comes to making a decision).

Always remember:

TRUST IN YOURSELF AND TRUST IN YOUR INSTINCTS.

5. *Don't Take Life So Seriously:*

Humor: "The quality of being pleasant, sympathetic, amusing or funny."

You may need to 'lighten up' and not take yourself and life so seriously. People are attracted to a sense of humor, and if you look at the definition above, then who wouldn't want to be like that, or be with someone who has those qualities. Nothing in life is as important as you think it is. It is said that 'every cloud has a silver lining', so whatever you perceive as being worth worrying or stressing over, the reality is that it really isn't. If you lose a job, then something else will turn up, if you lose a lover, then you will find another, if you get divorced, then being single will bring you new possibilities, if you get married, then you will get used to a new way of living and sharing your life …

Whether you choose Choice A or Choice B in life, it *will* work out for you! You may gain different experiences and different knowledge on each path, but when you have a relaxed attitude and an inner strength, you will always be satisfied at the eventual outcomes. It doesn't mean you are being blasé about your life, but more about being comfortable and being accepting with whatever happens to you.

As a result, whatever you encounter really isn't as bad or as serious as you may perceive it to be. When you lighten up, you learn, *things don't really matter as much as you think they do and that whatever happens to you, you will manage to handle it and deal with it appropriately!*

6. *Implement Your Decision:*

Once you have created the momentum and motivation you need, you will need to implement your decision and go through with it. Your actions should support your justifications as you develop the strength to move forwards and overcome any distractions and obstacles that come your way. Stand by your decision and be accountable for what choices you have made. Even if it feels difficult to start with, give it time and understand you made the best possible decision for yourself with all the relevant information you had available.

* Philip: "I feel so relieved that I finally made the decision to leave my wife. The relationship hadn't been working out for such a long time. We tried over and over again to make it work; we had so many discussions and arguments that in the end, I just felt so drained… In fact we both did. I tried my best for such a long time, we went to counselling, spoke with friends and even tried many different techniques that we both read about, but ultimately, we wanted different things. She wanted to have children, whereas I wanted us to travel and then start up our own business and work for ourselves. She really wasn't interested. Physically things weren't great between us either. I don't think we were truly compatible really. As hard as this split may be, I think it's best for the both of us. We love each other deep down, we just don't make each other happy anymore. I deliberated over this decision for such a long time, but now that I have made it, I feel I can move on and do what I need to. As for my wife, I know that in time she will find someone else who can make her happy and love her the way she needs to be loved. I feel very sad about it if I am being honest, but I also feel a huge sense of relief, as if a great weight has been lifted off my shoulders …"

AFTER MAKING A DECISION

1. *Forget Your Expectations:*

Once you have made and implemented your decision, then learn to live with it and change whatever expectations you have previously created. The future is out of your control, so just accept what transpires and follows, and adapt accordingly.

If you have created unrealistic expectations, then you may experience disappointment if you feel those expectations haven't come to/reached fruition. The problem then is that you may miss out on all the good experiences and opportunities that could come your way after you follow your new path. The reality can be that your new outcomes may be even better for you than what you had imagined, but because you are *so* focused on your original picture of what should have happened, you may miss out on all the new possibilities and opportunities that appear to you. In essence, don't get too focused on how it "should be" and focus more on how "it really is".

* Charlotte: "Once I left my old company, I was so disappointed that all the job interviews and opportunities I had been promised didn't happen. If it wasn't one problem, it was another. I was so sure I would get a new job after all the positive feedback that I received, that I was pretty deflated when I realised what the reality truly was. I then decided I would start up my own company as I couldn't wait forever for my 'dream job', so I looked into everything I needed to do, and then I just got on with it. I was always interested in fashion and have spent years helping people choose and wear clothes that suited them, so I took it one step further, and started working for myself as a 'Personal Stylist'. I advertised in local newspapers and at Women's Groups and Associations and before long, I had a very regular client base. I have now been contacted by one or two companies who have asked me to come in and help with their employees. From what I had originally pictured, my life has taken a weird and wonderful turn in a totally new, but greatly appreciated, direction ..."

2. *Be Accountable and Responsible For Your Decisions:*

As mentioned in the implementation stage of your decision making process, once you've carried it out, then be accountable and responsible for what you have decided.

Although this can be difficult, it's best not to blame anyone else for what happens in your life, but yourself. Living in *Denial* may be easier, but you learn nothing about life and keep repeating the same mistakes. Also, when you are accountable and responsible, you are less angry at people around you, as well as being less angry at yourself. Being able to find *opportunity* in any decision, means it's easier to accept *accountability* and *responsibly* for making it.

* Douglas: "I have no regrets in my life, because whatever has happened to me, I have decided to do it. No-one has forced me into doing anything and even if things don't work out the way I had planned, I learn from the experience, and move on quickly. In fact, if something doesn't work out, I know I will learn something new and bear that in mind for the next time. Life is for living, this isn't a dress rehearsal so what's the point in regretting anything or looking to blame others for what's happened to you. What you have to understand is that the common denominator for everything in your life is YOU! You are the one who chooses what to do, chooses your friends, chooses your partners and chooses where to go in life, so how can you possibly blame anyone else for your own shortcomings and misgivings. I don't believe anyone makes mistakes as such, because when you decide something, you use all the knowledge you have at that given moment, then you come up with something pertinent at that time.

I have made some difficult decisions in my life, such as living in different countries, starting my own businesses, investing in different things, letting go of people who have let me down, but overall, I am happy because I know I have been the '*master of my own destiny and the captain of my ship*'. I think my upbringing had a lot to do with it- I was always encouraged to do well and supported by my parents. I think my father was my greatest influence, because he never blamed anyone else in his life and he always said, "if you've got the intelligence, then use it", implying that you are responsible for making your own decisions and then accepting responsibility for what happens. That's the way I see life also ..."

3. *Don't Always Protect, Learn To Correct:*

Once you have decided what to do, then give it your best shot and go for it! However, if things don't work out the way you want, then don't be afraid to change things. It's never too late to turn things around, or find a new course of action which will be more beneficial for you. Just because you have deliberated over something, and come up with a decision, it doesn't mean you have to see it through to the end. Another good skill is knowing when to cut your losses, regroup, and realign the direction you are heading in. We touched on this in The Psychology of Making Decisions - *"we get attached to things that we ourselves have created."*

Be careful that you know the difference between cutting your losses and giving up too quickly or being too non-committed. Remember, it is important to know that you *don't like* something as well as knowing that you do like something. If you have truly committed yourself to something, tried your best, and then concluded that it's not for you, then that's also fine, just move onto something else that suits you better.

When you decide to move on from something, you will naturally be met with resistance and criticism even, from people in your life. E.g.:

"Are you sure you want to stop doing what you're doing and change careers? You've invested years building up your business, just think of all the time you've spent working on it and all the future money you may miss out on!"

175

Much was learned and experience was gained, so you may need to point out that nothing was a waste of time or money! At one point something may have been right for you, but if it no longer is, then it's time to move on and change what you do. If something is becoming a physical and emotional drain on you, then it is totally logical that you don't want to carry on with it anymore. After all, if it affects the quality of your life, then you need to remedy it, as soon as you can.

Not everything in life runs as smoothly as we hope it will. Sometimes we experience many difficulties and diversions along the way of our chosen path before we finally reach our goals. When we set out to do something, we envisage it to be simple in our mind's eye, maybe we see it as being like this in its simplicity:

A (Starting Point) > ---------- > --------- > --------- > B (Goal)

But the reality for us may be more like this:

A (Starting Point) > ---------- > (Difficulty) > ---------- > (Diversion) > --------- > (Confusion) > ---------- > (Re-evaluation) > ---------- > (Dissatisfaction) > --------- > (Correction) > ---------- > C (New Goal)

It's important not to worry about your decisions made because the key is *learning when and how to re-evaluate them!* Another important factor for you to bear in mind is *knowing* when to correct your decisions. Whenever you feel Confusion and Dissatisfaction in aiming for your original Goal, then these are the signals that maybe you need to correct what you are doing and create some clarity for yourself again. The whole point of making a decision is for it to lead you towards your Goals and leave you feeling proud with a sense of achievement. If at any point it creates too much negativity for you in terms of Difficulty, Confusion and Dissatisfaction, then your original Goal needs to be Re-evaluated and Corrected with a possible New Goal being the result.

Think of mental pain/turmoil as a signal that something needs to be changed in your life. If you suffered physically from any ailment or symptom, you would get it seen to and sorted out professionally. Learn to do the same with mental pain/turmoil: understand the symptoms and implement the necessary changes to create recovery for yourself emotionally and psychologically.

If you blindly follow the path that you have created and become oblivious to the changes you require, you will miss out on the help that you need, and ultimately also miss out on new opportunities and possibilities that would have come your way. Help can be in the form of support groups, friends, family, courses, self-help books, therapy or whatever else that you find as being beneficial for you.

Remember not to be closed and protective of what you have chosen, but to be open, ready to learn, and if need be, ready to correct your decisions also.

Review of steps:

WIN-WIN OUTCOME PROCESS

BEFORE MAKING A DECISION:

1). Focus on Your Win-Win Outcomes

2). Work Out Your Alternatives

3). Work Out Your Priorities

4). Follow Your Instinct

5). Don't Take Life so Seriously

6). Implement Your Decision

AFTER MAKING A DECISION:

1). Forget Your Expectations

2). Be Accountable and Responsible for Your Decisions

3). Don't Always Protect, Learn to Correct

You just have to be brave when it comes to making decisions and know that things can always be rectified one way or another. Every decision you make is an opportunity to learn, as is every "mistake". Whatever direction you head in through life, will bring you friends, experiences, possibilities, chances, partners, successes, etc., etc. You just have to have faith and belief that it will. Sometimes, the greatest gifts come from the least expected sources.

"The strongest people aren't always the people who win, but the people who don't give up when they lose."

Liam Payne

Changing direction and making corrections are an integral part of living. Somehow, we have been 'hoodwinked' into believing that we have to be perfect. This also applies to everything else in our lives- This misguided belief has meant we have all become fearful of being adventurous and suffer from trepidation at the very thought of trying out new concepts/ ideas/ techniques.

What you need to get your head around is the fact that not everything you do in life will be a success ... *that's a fact!* In reality, the more you attempt in life, statistically speaking, there will be a fifty percent chance of it not working out the way you envisage anyway! So what does that mean for you? That you will never try to get a job, never get involved in a relationship, never work for yourself, never experience new things.... Of course not, because life is for living, and that includes dealing with anything that you encounter along the way, however good or bad you may deem the results to be. Whether you can easily make decisions or not, the key is not to be fearful, and to also understand that whatever the outcome, your life *will* be enriched in one way or another.

Practicing Decision Making

Step One: Think over some of the decisions you are currently mulling over. Using the No-Lose/Win-Win Outcome model, make a note of ALL the positive outcomes that can result by making different choices, even if those outcomes aren't exactly what you had envisaged. This will present you with a list of everything positive that will come about irrespective of whichever direction you take.

Step Two: Create a mantra for yourself such as:

"IT MAKES NO DIFFERENCE!"

Every time you face a decision repeat that mantra to yourself. Start with the smaller daily decisions such as:

"Which outfit shall I wear today? = It makes no difference!"

"What shall I have for lunch? = It makes no difference!"

"Where shall I shop this evening? = It makes no difference!"

Whatever you choose will provide you with a different experience, and slowly you can learn to use this mantra and the ideology it represents for much larger and more important decisions.

Don't become overly fixated or obsessive in your life over anything. To help keep you grounded, remember to always say to yourself:

"IT MAKES NO DIFFERENCE!"

Step Three: Following on from the previous step, another good mantra you can use for yourself is:

"WHATEVER HAPPENS, I CAN DEAL WITH IT!"

Be strong, feel strong and use strong language to highlight the control you have over whatever happens to you in your life. Remain positive and carefree knowing that whatever occurs after you've made your decision, you are more than capable of dealing with it.

Step Four: Pay more attention to how you really feel about a decision you've made, and if you honestly feel things aren't working out for you, have the strength and belief to make the necessary changes to correct the situation. Remember, don't stubbornly continue with something that is bringing you no joy or benefit!

CHAPTER EIGHT:

OVERCOMING EMOTIONAL PROBLEMS

"We cannot solve our problems with the same thinking we used when we created them."

Albert Einstein

If you could define yourself, then how would you do it? Would you use only positive adjectives to describe yourself, or would you be able to see yourself as you truly are, 'warts and all'? For many of us, living in denial over certain aspects of our personalities, prevents us from developing and growing as adults. However, when we live in denial about how we truly are, unfortunately it affects us adversely in many areas of our lives. Interactions with family, friends, colleagues and partners all suffer because of our inability to address certain issues that we have. Unattractive personality traits such as resentment, neediness, constantly complaining, jealousy and anger, all stem from our *Dependency* on other people. These self-defeating traits are due to a deep-rooted *fear of losing someone (or something)* whom we see as the basis of our identity or existence even. Unfortunately, this type of dependency on other people/ other things shows a lack of self-reliance, and a neediness of others in an emotional or financial sense, for example.

Our mental and emotional filters seem to only let the positives through as they filter out anything negative in how we see ourselves. Try it. If you could describe yourself in five words, what would you say?

"I am: humorous, dependable, sympathetic, empathetic and loyal"

Or how about:

"I am: trustworthy, faithful, witty, intelligent and patient"

Maybe something along those lines would describe you best. Try it on other people. What would they say when describing themselves? Probably something similar, five *positive* adjectives with nothing negative … After all, who would describe themselves like this?

"I am: clingy, needy, overbearing, jealous and angry"

Not too many of us would describe ourselves like that it's safe to say. Yet if you think about it logically, it is impossible for us to be one hundred percent positive and zero percent negative. Yet as human beings, we know when it comes to 'selling ourselves', the best way to do it is by not being *too* honest. A fairer reflection would be a mix of positive and negative adjectives, but it's not human nature to accentuate anything negative. Just look at the dating sites and dating columns for proof of that:

"I am a 41yr old single man, 6'2" tall with an athletic physique, who's intelligent, open-minded, with a great sense of humor and an interesting job. I have many friends, like to travel, read, meet new people and I like to eat healthily and look after myself. I am close to my family and enjoy spending time with my parents. I am looking for a like-minded female to share my life with …"

"I am a 28 yr old fun loving girl who is loyal, faithful and trustworthy. I like going out with my friends and sharing good times together with them. I love to cook and enjoy a good glass of wine occasionally. Everyone describes me as kind, considerate and caring. Physically, I am attractive with blue eyes and mid-brown coloured hair. I am 5' 6" tall and am fairly sporty, with a curvy, athletic body. I am looking for someone to be my soul mate whom I can settle down with …"

Sound familiar? Add to these types of profiles a very flattering picture on dating sites, and watch the responses build up. Maybe this is natural when we are 'programmed' to look for positive traits in other people, as well as ourselves, but the danger is that it creates a deeper sense of *denial* in who we are as well as who other people truly are. This denial could cause us problems when it comes to how we view ourselves and how we view our relationships.

A more realistic picture of how we might think and how we may behave in certain relationships could look something like this:

* Salvatore: "I am devastated without Lisa, she meant everything to me. After ten years together, we are now divorcing and I am struggling to cope. I miss our young daughter and our life together. Lisa did everything for me: cooked, cleaned, washed my clothes, planned everything … She was my whole life really … What will I do without her?"

For Salvatore, Lisa *was* his whole life because that is exactly what he had made her. He had no friends or social life, and his whole existence was based around his wife. Nothing or no-one else had any meaning or significance for him. This explains his desperate sense of emptiness and devastation after his wife chose to divorce him. In many ways it also explains why his marriage broke down; His clingy and needy behaviour finally drove a wedge between him and his wife. She got sick and tired of his dependency on her. She felt more like his mother than his wife, and eventually, this led her to begin divorce proceedings. Maybe for Salvatore, therapy could have helped him see the reality of his situation, and how his emotional dependency on his wife was too overbearing for her. He couldn't see anything negative in his behaviour and this clearly led to the breakdown of his marriage.

For Salvatore, negative side effects accompanied his emotional dependency, and the same could be said for Anders, who chose to create his identity in the area of work. He was so career focused, that nothing else mattered. Also for Anders, fear and dependency meant that at work, instead of being open and expansive, he was closed and protective. He liked to seem important and took credit for everything in the office, ignoring the contributions of his colleagues. He was always careful in what he did, never taking chances in an effort to appease his superiors.

Unfortunately for Anders, due to cutbacks in the firm, he ended up losing his job, and as a result, he suffered an extreme sense of hopelessness and helplessness. He was left feeling devastated and empty by what had happened to him, and of course, what made it worse was the total lack of sympathy or empathy towards him from his colleagues. He finally understood the phrase about it being a, 'you reap what you sow' world. He received the same amount of consideration back as he had shown towards his colleagues. For Anders losing his job meant losing his identity, and he was left shrouded in negativity and despair by the whole experience.

Many men suffer when they lose their jobs or are forced to retire, the reason being that they are emotionally tied to their jobs throughout their lives. They invest a great deal of their time and energy into working, and many times, cannot see a life for themselves away from work. As a result, they miss out on all the opportunity and enjoyment that is still available to them. Of course, the above scenarios can also apply to women, but women are generally better at developing and maintaining friendships and networks, and are usually more creative in these situations than men are.

Let us look at another example of how emotional problems can manifest themselves:

* Rose was originally from the south of Europe. In the Mediterranean where she was from, family was *very* important. She was a housewife who stayed at home and made her children the *totality* of her life. She was always doing everything for everyone, and was desperate to be liked by people and to be seen as a good mother and person. She always defended her children no matter what, helped them out financially, and prided herself on caring *so much* for her children. Her whole world revolved around her children and what she could do for them.

What Rose couldn't see or comprehend, was that she had created a scenario whereby her children had become her reason to exist. Another thing that Rose was oblivious to, was the negative side-effects her behaviour was causing and perpetuating: her need to control, her need to dominate, her overbearing protectiveness, her justifications for being self-righteous, and the massive amounts of guilt and dependency that *she* was creating in her own children. She always made it clear to them how much she had sacrificed for them and how much she had given them while they were growing up … and she continued to do so even after they had grown up and left home.

This type of behaviour is damaging on so many levels:

Parents like this suffer immense feelings of emptiness when their children eventually fly the nest. They are not sympathetic or empathetic to the needs of their partners. They create a long term detrimental relationship with their children because they depend on their children for their own emotional strength and survival. These over-powering dependencies place a continued emotional burden on their children throughout their lives. The children are left constantly feeling indebted or guilty (either consciously or subconsciously) whenever they interact with their parents.

In all of the above examples, whether it relates to a spouse, work or children, you can see many negative emotional problems that result from the relationships that have been created. When each person has lost the thing that they most identify with, it has exposed their clingy and needy behaviour, together with a whole host of other negative emotional difficulties for them. No doubt at some point in your life, you also have suffered the type of emotional problems and difficulties faced by Salvatore, Anders and Rose. When you feel that desperate in your life, it can be one of the most painful experiences you are likely to suffer. To make matters worse, when you have those helpless and hopeless feelings, it can leave you in the throes of anxiety where you struggle to see a way out for yourself.

What can you do to rid yourself of all the negative emotions that a loss can inflict on you?

Firstly, you need to understand that to implement change, you will need a great deal of awareness, patience, perseverance and understanding to break strong emotion-backed patterns. It may not be easy, but if you take precise and manageable steps, then change is possible for you. After all, if your goal is to rid yourself of negative emotions such as, desperation, emptiness, fear, hopelessness, neediness, etc, then with action and commitment, you will absolutely be able to change the quality of your life for the better.

When your life is out of balance, then it becomes clear to see how empty it truly is and how this emptiness will leave you with an array of negative emotions and feelings.

We can look at the three main areas of your life, which we have already touched on: Relationships, Work and Children (Family). If we take one of them, Work for example, we can see what your life will look like if you focus your emotions and energies in one area only.

LIFE WITH WORK = COMPLETE

LIFE WITHOUT WORK = EMPTY

The same can be said of the other two areas, for example:

LIFE WITH CHILDREN = COMPLETE

LIFE WITHOUT CHILDREN = EMPTY

LIFE WITH A RELATIONSHIP = COMPLETE

LIFE WITHOUT A RELATIONSHIP = EMPTY

When your life is empty without the thing that occupies it completely, you become *desperate* to replace what is lost. That is why so many people jump from one relationship to another, because their lives are so unfulfilled and empty when they don't have a relationship to focus on. The same applies when people lose their jobs; they become so desperate to work sometimes, that they take any job, even if it's totally unsuitable for them. As mentioned earlier, that is also why parents feel so helpless and empty when their children finally leave home- they have nothing left, but a huge, empty void.

What is a better way to view your life? Below is an example of a more *Fulfilling Life*:

LIFE WITH WORK = FAMILY, FRIENDS, LEISURE TIME, ALONE TIME, HOBBIES, PERSONAL GROWTH, RELATIONSHIP, *WORK*.

LIFE WITHOUT WORK = FAMILY, FRIENDS, LEISURE TIME, ALONE TIME, HOBBIES, PERSONAL GROWTH, RELATIONSHIP.

When you create a fulfilling life for yourself with many different areas and facets, then work is just *one* part of your life, and not the *only* thing you live for. As mentioned, the same can be said for having children or having a relationship in your life (this can also relate to having friends or having anything else for that matter).

With many different resources available to you, your life will be fulfilling with options and abundance, and as a result, your neediness and dependency will dissipate. Of course, if a certain aspect of your life is no longer available for you, you may be sad and feel some pain because of its absence, but when your life is 'whole', it will still be able to function fairly normally until what's missing can be replaced when you are ready and willing for that to happen.

It's important you commit to each area of your life and try to keep it as balanced as possible. That way, you will be able to maintain the right level of equilibrium and not over compensate for what is or isn't in your life. What may sometimes happen if your life is not in the right balance is that you place too much emphasis in a certain area. For example, let us say that you have a fairly fulfilling life with all the necessary areas of your life in balance according to you. You may in reality place too much emphasis on *one* area, such as your relationship, and if it were to unfortunately end, you would be lost as all the other areas of your life would not be sufficient enough for you to function normally. The same can be said for other areas, such as work; people who place too much emphasis and attention on work are totally at a loss if they find themselves without a job.

For people with a total imbalance in their lives, they suffer terribly with their emotions when they lose the major component of their existence. They can get depressed, feel desperate and even feel suicidal when the loss leads to an impending emptiness with 'no way out'.

To help you maintain the right levels of commitment to each area of your life, you need to create high levels of awareness, perseverance and patience to what is happening to you in your environment.

188

How do you create commitment in each area of your life?

You need to consciously give 100% of your time and energy when you are engaged in whatever area of your life you are involved with at the time. For example, if you are with your family, you need to totally focus on them, and give all your focus and energy to your interactions with them. If you are with your partner, again, focus your energies on your time together and engage 100% with each other. The same rule applies when you are with your friends, or when you are exercising, or when you are working, and so on. Whatever situation and area you find yourself in, don't let your focus and mind wander off to something or someone else. In this day and age it is a lot more difficult because almost everyone has a mobile phone and is on social networking sites, so it is quite natural to be constantly distracted, but if you want truly fulfilling relationships, you must learn to control your urges to become distracted and draw energy away from what/who you are involved with at that particular time. Be honest, how do you feel when you are with someone and they are constantly looking at their phone/responding to texts and mails/making calls every few minutes/interrupting their time with you by bringing other people into your interaction ….

When you can commit your energies to exactly where it needs to be used, then the quality of your life will improve no-end. Each area of your life will get the attention it deserves and you will get the most out of *every* situation and interaction you find yourself in. Also, if an area of your life is suddenly taken away from you, after the initial difficulty, you will manage to cope with it and overcome it. You also need to create the correct balance between being in the real world and the 'virtual' world. More and more people are suffering from major psychological problems because of their on-line addictions. Although technology has improved the quality of our lives dramatically, it has also lead to an increase in addictions, obsessions and compulsive behaviors which have been connected to the use of technology. ***This is because of our inability to remain focused and committed to the important areas of our lives.***

What can you do to enhance the concept of Commitment?

Change the way you see yourself by using the following tool: Every time you are in any given situation, *"focus on it 100% and act as if you really count in the world"*. What this implies is that instead of seeing yourself as insignificant, see yourself as being *meaningful* and *important*. This results in:

- You creating a more positive environment for yourself in whatever area, scenario or situation you find yourself in.

- You interacting with people in a way that would make *their* day happier.

- You creating daily goals for yourself and making sure you accomplish them.

- You participating 100% in everything that you do.

The above results will eliminate any boredom you may be feeling in your life, as well as increasing your levels of positivity and satisfaction. When you start "focusing 100% and acting as if you really count in the world", you begin to believe and see that you really can make a difference in your environment. Also other positives for you are an increased level of self-esteem, and a genuine sense of empowerment due to your heightened commitment levels.

Most people think of *commitment* as a duty or restriction in some way, but it doesn't necessarily have to be a heavy concept. Also, for most people, it represents something that lasts 'forever', and that is part of the reasoning for those who suffer from a commitment phobia. Therefore they become scared to commit to anything, because they feel that commitment is a burden, a long lasting and restrictive process … A process which they feel they will ultimately not live up to, and fail.

The thing about committing to anything, be it work or a relationship for example, is that it doesn't necessarily mean that it will last forever. By nature, *nothing* lasts forever. Commitment merely means engaging in something 100% while you are involved in it, be it work, or a relationship, or life itself. No-one really knows how long anything will last, but you owe it to yourself to show your life the dignity and respect it deserves by committing 100% to everything you are involved in. Sadly, some things in life will come to an end that may be out of your control. This can involve work, friendships, relationships, etc. When something does end, if you have given it 100% and done your best, then you will have NO regrets. Although the loss may be enormous at the time, it will not be overriding as you will have many other areas in your life that you are committed 100% to.

Another important area to look at which has not been mentioned thus far is *Value*. Just how much value would you say that you add/contribute to other people's lives? If you can honestly say that your existence adds value to the lives of everyone you meet, then you will already know the benefits it provides to your self-esteem and sense of self-worth. Simply note that by making a difference to other people and their lives, the *Value* that you contribute actually comes back to you. The 'feel good factor' that you help to create is mutually beneficial.

Understanding the idea behind creating a *fulfilling life* for yourself will enable you to see how much it can help you reduce and overcome common emotional problems such as, anxiety, fear, stress and worry.

Here are five steps that can help you focus to do this:

Step 1

This step involves a little soul searching and finding some 'home-truths' about yourself. If you look carefully at your life, you will notice that every time you have suffered negative feelings derived from loss, you have taken the very same steps in your efforts to relieve the emptiness. You have tried to re-capture the very thing that you have lost, by substituting the old with the new. In reality, you may have created and helped perpetuate a vicious circle for yourself.

LOSS > EMPTINESS > NEW SUBSTITUTE > VICIOUS CIRCLE

This way of being can easily be demonstrated when most people's relationships end. Instead of remaining single for a period of time and working out what went wrong or what they truly want in a relationship, they go out and find another person to be with. They substitute the old relationship with a new person. The strange thing is that they continue with their old patterns of behaviour and expect the new relationship to work out differently. Invariably, it doesn't! After splitting from the new paramour, then guess what, they go out and find another person and repeat the process all over again. This pattern of behaviour can define whole lifestyles for some people.

If this pattern sounds familiar to you, then the key is to firstly *Recognize* what you are doing. Understand you did not have an appropriate framework for yourself to create a healthier way to behave. This is important because by doing this, you are not being too harsh on yourself or blaming yourself for past errors of judgment or misdemeanors that you may have carried out. By understanding yourself a little more, and recognizing that you can behave in another way, it will lead you onto the next step.

Step 2

Create a *fulfilling life* for yourself! We looked earlier at what a more fulfilling life for you may look like, with many other different areas to focus on, and not with just one predominant area. When you have some quiet time for yourself, write down

192

at least seven or eight areas of your life that you could invest more time in, which would ultimately bring more joy, satisfaction and value for you. You could include the areas already mentioned, or think up other areas that are more relevant for you.

Step 3

This step involves Visualization. Remember, you have to 'see it to be it'. Once you have a list of areas that you need to incorporate into your life, focus on them one at a time, by closing your eyes, and picturing what you would like that part of your life to look like. Using the two concepts of, '*Focusing and Acting as if you really count in the world*' together with '*100% Commitment*', ask yourself the following questions:

- 'How would these new behaviors feel for me?'

- 'How would I be interacting with the people in my life?'

- 'How would I view my environment?'

- 'What are the new things that I would be doing?'

Step 4

When you start to envisage and see clearly what your mind has created for you, then write all these things down as a confirmation of what you have visualized. Pay particular attention to all the finer details, such as how you speak, the words you use, how you move, how you feel and so forth. Imagine yourself in your new role carrying out everything that you have created. Then imagine being able to see yourself behaving in this more optimal way of being.

<u>Step 5</u>

The final step requires focus and action. Write down the many things that you would need to do in order for your visualization to become your Reality. Again, be meticulous and careful as you think through *everything* that you need to do. Your abilities to focus and then be proactive are critical in making your real life match your visualization.

FOCUS AND ACTION ARE THE KEYS TO BEING SUCCESSFUL.

<u>In reality, how would these steps work for you?</u>

Whichever area of your life you visualize wanting to improve, then this is how you would implement it. Let us say you would like to focus and be proactive in improving the area of Friendship, start by then being 100% committed, 'focusing and acting as if you really count in the world ...' Be committed to being with your friends, so when you are with them, you focus on them and find pleasure and fulfilment in their presence. Don't disrespect a friend by treating him/her as a "Super-Sub". In other words, don't make your friends feel they are being called upon when *you* have nothing better to do in your life. When your date cancels last minute, or when someone else lets you down, don't call on Super-Sub to help you when you feel needy or desperate. Of course you could say that's what friends are for, but that is being disrespectful to them, and at the same time, if you are being a Super-Sub in your life, then show yourself some respect by not being at someone else's beck and call when it suits them. Friendship is about healthy participation on both sides. It's not about creating needy and clingy attachments and treating people as a last minute replacement for relationship problems or other life problems.

If you visualized yourself as being an optimal friend, how would that look for you?

You might see yourself as sending a text or calling them to see how they are; meeting up with them for a drink/lunch/dinner; sending them a card, letter or email to acknowledge your appreciation; being more helpful; sharing good times together; being more proactive in your interactions rather than waiting for them to contact you … In other words, you wouldn't be disrespectful, needy, envious or jealous of people you regard as being your friends.

If you would like to focus and be proactive in another area of your life, such as Personal Growth, then you might visualize yourself as taking courses, reading self-help books, finding a suitable mentor, downloading relevant information, etc. Again, being 100% committed, 'focusing and acting as if you count in the world', mean that you will remain active, assured and focused in reaching your goals.

Let us say you picture yourself doing a course, then you might see yourself doing all the coursework and homework, interacting with other students, passing all the exams, happily looking forward to gaining your diploma, etc, etc. As before, when you close your eyes and visualize yourself doing this, then the chances of it becoming your reality are vastly improved.

Whatever area of your life you choose to focus on, don't be discouraged when old habits return, because whatever stage of development you are at, you will quite naturally want to practice what is most familiar to you. Old habits are like a comfortable old coat that is difficult to take off and easy to put on again. However far you feel you are moving forwards, there will always be periods where you will naturally wander away from your commitment, therefore you need to be ultra-vigilant. Eventually you will be able to focus totally on your commitment, and as a result your confidence and self-esteem will also receive a massive boost.

Once your self-esteem receives a boost, you learn to become more self-sufficient also and your neediness then begins to disappear. The problem with being needy is that you struggle to understand your surroundings and struggle to grow from your life-experiences, resulting in you starving yourself emotionally.

Let us look at another area of your life that you maybe need to commit more energy to – your leisure time. If you are overly focused on work and achievement, then you may find it difficult to just enjoy yourself and relax. Indeed, many people suffer from an inability to unwind and to be relaxed, and for some people, the idea of trying to relax makes them feel anxious in itself. Maybe when you are with your friends and your partner, it may be easier for you to enjoy your leisure time. However, the real problem for you could be when you are on your own you feel you should be occupying yourself and trying to accomplish something with your free-time. Again, the best way to release the anxiety you may be feeling when you're alone and trying to do something for yourself is to keep focused on being 100% committed to your leisure and relaxation time. Be aware of what you are doing and immerse yourself wholeheartedly into your chosen activity. Also, 'act as if you are meaningful in your life' and believe that your leisure time and relaxation time really count for something regarding your emotional well-being and your overall health.

Sometimes it is difficult to just relax. If you are used to working at a high tempo and your mind is constantly engaged, then as you can imagine, it will be difficult for you to just 'switch off'. When your mind works this way, then you have to introduce some routine in your leisure time also. If your work day consists of meetings, deadlines and dealing with stressful situations, then you really need to structure your leisure time, because this is the way your mind is geared. Just doing nothing or trying to relax can feel forced for you. You can create structure by giving your free-time activities some routine and deadlines also. You may need to think like this:

9 a.m. – 11 a.m.:- Read newspapers/magazines; read articles on your tablet/computer

11 a.m. – 12 p.m.:- Go for a walk/exercise

12 p.m. – 1 p.m.:- Have lunch

1 p.m. – 3 p.m.:- Paint/Write/Do Photography (or any other hobby)

3 p.m. – 5 p.m.:- Go out shopping and window shop/ have a coffee/ buy something if you desire

5 p.m. – 9 p.m.:- Meet friends for dinner

10 p.m. onwards:- Relax and enjoy the company of family

If you have a free day, as above, then you can give it some structure to help you focus on doing beneficial things for your psychological well-being. Even on a work day, you can include activities that will enable you to 'zone out' and do something to help you relax. Using your leisure time in a more optimal way (either daily or hourly) will also help your mind de-clutter, and help you find better ideas and insights.

It is important to bear in mind that whatever you commit to doing and whichever areas you commit to improving, with the necessary focus and action, they can become your reality.

Every day you need to focus on accomplishing your daily goals, and then diligently you need to follow the correct steps to achieve them. In reality, you probably already have this mindset when it comes to work. The important thing is to be diligent in other areas of your life also, and to create the balance that you need.

Each of your goals should be approached with *100% commitment* and with an *'I count'* mentality. These attributes will heighten your focus and sense of fulfilment in helping you to achieve. Of course, what you are really trying to achieve in your life is overall balance. There will be times when you may need to use more of your energy in a certain area of your life at a certain time. For example, sometimes your relationship will require more of your attention, whilst at other times work demands may require more of your energy and focus... Apart from these specific periods, always remember, *Balance is the Key!*

What type of Emotional Problems should you be aware of?

Anxiety:

Anxiety occurs if you think there may be some kind of threat for/to you. Anxious thoughts are usually connected to future events – often when 'what if ...' thoughts are apparent in your thinking. You may be worried about social situations such as a fear of rejection, or you may be fearful of physical danger such as a fear of having a heart attack. The degree of your anxiety is determined by two things:

I) On *How threatening* you deem the situation to be for you

II) Your confidence in your *own ability* to cope with the situation

Think of anxiety like an over-sensitive alarm system which overestimates danger and underestimates your coping resources. As a result you may seek constant reassurance from other people, avoid social situations, and this may also be a significant contributing factor to your procrastination over decisions.

There may be a tendency for you to over-estimate the probability of bad things happening, and this results in you making incorrect evaluations. Another problem of anxious thinking is that you focus on negatives and perceived threats rather than being able to see any positive aspects.

Anxiety problems tend to fall into patterns of disorder, and each disorder is characterized by certain types of anxious thinking. The following disorders can all be related to anxiety:

Panic Disorders; Agoraphobia; Social Phobias; Generalized Anxiety Disorders; and other Simple Phobias.

One of the main problems with anxiety based disorders, is that it creates 'self-fulfilling prophecies' for you. Your beliefs lead you to behave in a way that elicit a negative response from others, thus 'proving' what you believe to be true. Another negative for you, is that you confirm your maladaptive beliefs by selecting 'evidence' that agrees with your negative thoughts and maladaptive thinking. Overall though, anxiety may also be a secondary feature to other major problems, such as depression, for example.

Depression

Many people use the word 'depression' to describe a mood state or feelings of a 'low mood'. However, the deeper sense of depression refers to a series of symptoms which form a prolonged pattern of behaviour.

What do you need to watch out for in regards to the symptoms of depression?

- Behavioral: Reduced coping, social skills deficits, decreased activity.

- Motivational: Apathy, loss of energy, loss of interest.

- Biological: Loss of appetite, sleep disturbance, decreased physical performance.

- Cognitive: Negative thinking, poor concentration, being indecisive.

- Affective: Anger, anxiety, depressed mood, guilt.

A significant area to be wary of is negative thinking, which is a prominent part of depression. If you feel unable to alter your life situation, and feel unhappy about the situation you find yourself in, you could be suffering from depression. Another clue is that you cannot see how things can change in the future. You may also tend to focus on the 'theme of loss' or 'a failure to achieve a desired goal'. Common areas that can lead to depression are connected to relationships: a marriage break-up (loss), or a bad relationship (failure to achieve a desired goal).

Below are some examples of specific types of negative thinking. Do you say or think any of the following?

- "What's the point?"; "It's not worth trying." (Apathy)

- "I will never find another person as good as he was/ she was." (Depressed Mood)

- "I just can't cope with it anymore." (Reduced Coping)

Other extremely negative behaviour patterns to look out for are:

- Guilt (whereby you think you have done something wrong and then exacerbate this by believing you are a bad person).

- Suicidal Thoughts (whereby you feel totally hopeless and see your life as unbearable with no possibility of your circumstances changing in the future).

If you feel you are suffering from anxiety or depression, then by using the tools in this book and other self-help books, you will be able to gradually work through your problems. Of course, some sessions of Counselling/Therapy may also be recommended for you to help you list the various symptoms you are experiencing, and then to tackle them one at a time (for example, depressed moods, hopelessness and inactivity). If you can learn to realistically appraise your problems, rather than seeing them as catastrophic, you are far less likely to be paralyzed by your problems, and you'll be more likely to face up to them and try to deal with them.

Shame, Guilt and Anger

These negative emotions can be the manifestation of anxiety problems, depression and other emotional difficulties.

If you experience a lot of shame and embarrassment, then you are probably extremely sensitive about what other people think about you. You also may get anxious in social situations. Feelings of shame for you are triggered when:

I) Other people observe you 'breaking a social rule'.

II) You infer that those watching you are making negative evaluations about what you have done.

III) You apply the negative evaluations to yourself.

When you are observed to break a social rule, you tend to see yourself as being weak, incompetent and inferior, and it's these feelings that lead you to feeling shame.

Embarrassment is similar to shame, but is milder in that, although the same type of thinking processes occur, you may not feel as weak, incompetent and inferior as you would do if you felt shame. However, the central thinking processes for both emotions are that you feel the negative evaluations that you have inferred that others have made about you, are true. Therefore, self-devaluation is prominent to feelings of shame and embarrassment.

Physical symptoms of shame and embarrassment are: Looking down; avoiding eye contact; a desire to be away from public view; blushing; negative feelings; future avoidance of triggers.

Guilt

Maybe if you are suffering from anxiety or depression, another negative emotion connected to that would be guilt. Guilt occurs when you feel that you have done something morally wrong; you feel you have violated your moral code or your own standards in some capacity. Guilt in itself is what we all feel at some point or another; but deeper feelings of guilt are attached to you if you feel that you are a 'bad person'.

If you feel 'pathological guilt' in this way, then you may react in a number of ways which will compound your problems. These 'maladaptive reactions' include:

I) You may try to mend the wrongs in an unproductive way, for example you may desperately beg for forgiveness in these types of situation, and then you may end up hating yourself for behaving in such a degrading manner.

II) You may even berate yourself and then resort to self-punishment as a result. You may feel that as you have done something awful, you are a 'bad person', and therefore you deserve punishment. The danger here is that you may end up doing yourself serious physical or psychological damage because of the punishment/self-harm you have inflicted on yourself.

III) If you're suffering from deeper feelings of guilt (anxiety/depression), you may try to drown or block out negative feelings by using alcohol or other drugs. These may cure the problem short-term, but long-term will create another whole host of physiological problems for you.

IV) Guilt also brings about denial, whereby you may end up not taking responsibility for your actions, and you may end up blaming others for what you have done. In fact, lack of responsibility and 'passing the buck' are common defense mechanisms of people suffering from guilt.

V) You may not be able to focus on avoiding the problem in the future, instead, you focus on achieving forgiveness from others, or you continue to berate yourself. You also may make unrealistic promises to yourself such as, "I promise I will never do it again …" without attempting to understand the factors which led you to behave that way in the first place. This makes it difficult for you to keep your promises, and you end up repeating the problematic behaviour again.

If you suffer deeper feelings of guilt, you may also suffer from feelings of being selfish. Your guilt makes you focus on trying to be unselfish, and paradoxically, this preoccupation with being unselfish, may lead you to being *even more* preoccupied with yourself, and inhibit you from being assertive and being sensitive to the needs of others.

Anger

In reality, anger is an emotion that is the manifestation of other negative feelings, such as frustration. If we feel frustrated at something, be it other people, circumstances, ourselves, etc., then how we control this frustration is the key to whether it develops further or not. If we can't control the feelings of frustration, then they develop into anger because of our perceived feelings of injustice at *not getting* what we had hoped for, or because we feel something *should not* have happened (but has). If we feel angry at someone or something, we look to blame them or damn them for causing us to feel the way we do. The problem is that this 'damning attitude' is not conducive to us being able to express ourselves in a constructive manner.

After all, if you *lose your temper,* then as is suggested, you have *lost* control of the situation and *lost* control of your behaviour. Therefore, *Anger equates to a loss of your faculties*.

Possible Sources of Anger for You:

I) If you are blocked from achieving a certain valued goal, this can lead to dysfunctional anger such as you demanding to yourself that the *frustration absolutely should not have occurred*. The valued goal to be achieved can be anything in range from a train you usually catch being cancelled, to missing out on a promotion.

II) You may also suffer from anger if you feel that you have broken certain personal rules. If you strongly believe that you should be treated a certain way by others for example, then if you are not treated as you want to be, it will lead to you getting angry. These personal rules you have created may include being treated politely, with fairness, with consideration and with *respect*. It may be more realistic to realise that you cannot always be treated the way you *expect* to be treated by everyone that you encounter, especially when you feel disrespected.

III) Another source of anger is known as 'self-defense anger'. It stems from your self-esteem being compromised/threatened by the responses of another person or organisation. If you feel criticized in some way, you become defensive by getting angry, and this anger protects you from negative self-evaluation. This may be a normal response for you, if you are a defensive or 'touchy' person, or if you find it difficult to accept responsibility. The reason you get angry, is because the alternative for you by accepting responsibility, means it equates to you being worthless or a failure. Therefore, rather than evaluating a situation, seeing if you are at fault, apologizing if need be, and learning, you may choose to get angry to deflect any criticism from you.

The consequences of anger for you are that you may end up attacking or retaliating against your perceived cause of frustration. You could behave passive-aggressively by being awkward and un-cooperative, or you could be more direct by being verbal or physical. If you feel victimized, then you may respond to situations in a more aggressive and destructive manner. Being consumed by anger over a long period of time can be very self-destructive for you. Psychologically, angry thinking can dominate your thoughts and prevent you from enjoying life. Physiologically, anger can have serious consequences on your health and result in you suffering from high blood pressure, for example.

To increase the levels of satisfaction in your life and to help you in your continued growth as a person, you need to set up the basic structures to be able to do so. You need to be responsible for your actions and your behaviour, and you need to be able to recognize when and how to change if need be.

Remember, **"If you do what you've always done, you'll get what you've always gotten."**

Don't be afraid in looking for help if that is beneficial for you. Mentors, coaches, counsellors or support groups are all helpful sources that can help you recognize your weak points and can provide the resources that are needed to correct and build your character to where you need it to be. *It is important to know what you want and how to get it.*

Once you have implemented the necessary steps in your life, it will provide you with the determination that you need to change into a calmer and more balanced individual.

CHAPTER NINE

ACCEPTANCE AND FULFILLMENT

"Happiness cannot come from without. It must come from within …"

Helen Keller

As difficult as everything may be for you in your life, the fundamental concept of your existence should be *Acceptance*. Instead of living in denial with regard to your own environment and living in denial with regard to your own behavior, *Accept* who you are, what your role is, and what it has been throughout your life.

Sometimes our lives take on a direction seemingly out of our control. We can't always determine where we are heading and why. Our lives, and those of others seem to have a 'flow' or a 'force' that can change direction at any time due to an unexpected turn of events. The problem for most people, is that unexpected equates to *fear*… And fear means expecting the *worst* in outcomes. An important belief and idea to hold on to is that:

ACCEPTANCE IS THE ANTIDOTE TO OUR FEARS

Acceptance means affirming and agreeing to whatever hand life deals us. Once we can do this, and let go of resistance, then we become open to new opportunities and new possibilities as we enable ourselves to see our environment in a new way. By being calmer to our surroundings, we can reduce our levels of anxiety and stress. If you find it difficult to Accept, then you perpetuate your feelings of being a victim. The "How could this possibly happen to me?" mentality means that you block and resist your opportunities of growth and personal development. Living in denial creates emotional difficulty, exhaustion, tension and wasted energy in your life. Even worse, it creates apathy and inactivity. Following on from the last chapter, by saying, "I can't cope; I can't continue like this; There is no hope …" you continue to perpetuate your life of living in denial. Only Acceptance can counteract what holds you back in your life …

Not only is Acceptance your antidote to dealing with your day-to-day disappointments, fears, missed opportunities and rejections, *it is also vital in helping you deal with your greatest challenges and your deepest fears, throughout your life.*

Acceptance is a commonly used expression and ideology, but what does it really mean?

Firstly, let us look at a definition of Acceptance:

"Acceptance in human psychology is a person's assent to the reality of a situation, recognizing a process or condition (often a negative or uncomfortable situation) without attempting to change it, protest, or exit. The concept is close in meaning to 'acquiescence', derived from the Latin 'acquiesce' (to find rest in).

Acceptance is fundamental to the core dogma of most Abrahamic religions, the word "Islam" can be translated as "acceptance", "surrender" or "voluntary submission" and Christianity is based upon the "acceptance" of Jesus of Nazareth as the "Christ" and could be compared to some Eastern religious concepts such as Buddhist mindfulness. Religions and psychological treatments often suggest the path of acceptance when a situation is both disliked and unchangeable, or when change may be possible only at great cost or risk. **Acceptance** may imply only a lack of outward, behavioral attempts at possible change, but the word is also used more specifically for a felt or hypothesized cognitive or emotional state.

Beliefs and acceptance overlap, however they can be very diverse. The acceptance of ones beliefs is important to show commitment and structure of one's life. Not only is it vital for survival, it is a utility that is used in everyday relationships. For a single person to be accepted from a friend of theirs has shown to have an impact on an individual's self-esteem and well-being. In fact, without the acceptance, it could lead to a host of psychological issues."

Wikipedia

E. Tolle (Power of Now), defines acceptance as a "this is it" response to anything occurring in any moment of life. 'There, strength, peace and serenity are available when one stops struggling to resist, or hang on tightly to what is so in any given moment. What do I have right now? Now what am I experiencing? The point is, can one be sad when one is sad, afraid when afraid, silly when silly, happy when happy, judgmental when judgmental, over thinking when over thinking, serene when serene, etc.'

_____

Now that we have looked at a definition of Acceptance, let's look at some examples of how it works in peoples' lives:

* Curtis was born and grew up in a tough part of East London. He was in a gang throughout his formative years and was always in trouble one way or another. He enjoyed his 'hard man' persona which served him well, until he was injured in a street fight. Unfortunately for Curtis, the injuries he sustained were very bad and left him in a wheelchair.

After that, because of his disability, he lost all hope. Whereas before, he was reliant on his physical strength and imposing physique, he was now reduced to being cared for by other people. He found everything very difficult to deal with and was close to giving up on many occasions. The turning point for him came when he was at his lowest point. During a counselling session, he came to the realization that he could either *accept* his fate, or live in anger and denial as he spiraled further and further into depression. He chose to accept his situation and look at ways to make his life more fulfilling.

Once he chose to accept what had happened to him, his progress was quite remarkable. New opportunities opened up to him, possibilities that he never thought about before. Acceptance led to him to see that his existence could have a new purpose: To help young people with difficulties in their lives, and also those who were involved in gangs. He would be a mentor and help them see that there was an alternative. In a strange way, for Curtis, for the first time in his life, he began to think about *other people* and how to help them, instead of thinking about himself, and what *he* could get from other people. It took his disability to make him see that he actually had something to offer and contribute to the world, instead of seeing the world as a place that he could exploit and use to his own advantage.

Before his disability, Curtis had lived a selfish existence and was oblivious to the fact that his life had any deeper meaning or purpose. By *accepting* what had happened to him, it enabled him to move forward and escape the anger of being helpless and living in limbo. He now realizes his life before his disability was ironically futile in many ways. Maybe the catalyst for creating deeper satisfaction in his life was the one thing that he thought was the most dreadful.

* Anna felt immense pain and loss when her husband passed away. She was totally reliant on him for almost every aspect of her life. She also missed the warmth, strength and companionship that she gained from being with him. For a long time she really struggled emotionally and psychologically to understand what had happened to her life as she knew it. There was an emptiness and void which seemed all consuming for her, as she struggled to come to terms with what had happened. Finally, she began to *accept* that her life would change forever, and that things would never be the same again. This realization meant that she understood she needed to transform herself from being dependent to being independent. By being left to her own resources, her sense of self-esteem eventually increased to a very high level as she slowly learned to do things she had never done before. By finally accepting what had happened to her and the situation she found herself in, Anna was finally able to create a whole new life and a fulfilling existence for herself.

Bereavement is an extremely painful process. It takes a long time for the pain to eventually stop, but what you unfortunately end up learning, is that in life, there are a lot of 'goodbyes', and nothing can ever change that for you. If you can at some point accept death as an inevitability, you will find fulfillment in knowing how blessed you were to have had that person in your life. Mourning is a natural process with no time scale, and you can only get to the level of acceptance when you have gone through the whole mourning process (Denial, Anger, Bargaining, Depression/Grief, and *Acceptance*). However much you miss someone, there are three important things to understand:

1) Acceptance leads you to the realization that the person you mourn for always wanted the best for you, no matter what.

2) Acceptance leads you to the realization that whoever you have lost *lives on in you* in some capacity, with their beliefs, hopes, and ideas.

3) Acceptance leads you to the realization that the person you have lost wants you to be happy in your life and to live your life to its fullest.

Bereavement is probably the hardest and most difficult thing that we all have to go through in our lives. We can't always explain our pain to other people, and until we experience this pain ourselves, we can't truly understand the magnitude of death and the deep sense of loss and pain that it evokes.

ACKNOWLEDGEMENT OF PAIN IS VITAL; DENIAL IS DEADLY.

To analyze, your ability to function and cope effectively in this world corresponds to your ability to accept whatever hand fate has dealt you, however painful that may be.

What are the consequences of not Accepting?

Unacknowledged pain can subtly destroy your life. If you keep it submerged and live in denial, it can be very destructive. If you become out of touch with the pain you are suffering. If you have refused to let yourself feel negative emotions. If you have refused not to acknowledge your pain, then all this can manifest itself into a physical symptom/illness or into self-destructive levels of anger. By accepting something difficult, however painful it may be, then not only do you become resilient, but you also gain a life-lesson (that's if you choose to look for it. Remember "seek and you shall find").

* Derrick was a very self-centered and abusive man. His wife tolerated his behaviour for years until she gathered the strength to finally leave him. Derrick then struggled to cope with his wife divorcing him and taking their son from him. He

had always dabbled in drugs and alcohol, but after his wife left him, he spiraled out of control into a maelstrom of self-pity and also wallowed in his "woe is me" attitude. He refused to accept his levels of responsibility and culpability for his behaviour and actions. He continued to blame everyone else for the negativity in his life and refused to see the many opportunities, possibilities and blessings in his life. Many of his friends who had remained loyal to him, eventually gave up on him, as they too struggled to cope with his destructive behaviour. The pain of living in denial and not accepting the consequences of his behaviour made it impossible for him to see the part he played in the outcomes in his life. He remained an angry man who continued to drink too much alcohol, and take too many drugs in his efforts to self-medicate.

* Amber was a woman who lived her life in a very self-centered and egotistical way. She always thought about herself first and had little regard or respect for other people. She was involved in many financial scams and often treated family members with contempt as she tricked them out of their money. She also fraudulently deceived organisations out of their money. She met her partner Martin (who was also a 'scam-artist'), and together their common interest of 'making money' united them. Eventually they fell out over money, and Amber's health began to deteriorate not long after. She became extremely angry and vengeful towards Martin because she felt she was deceived by him, yet the irony was she couldn't see that he had done to her what she had done to other people. The *angrier* she became, the more her health suffered. By living her life in a very negative manner and having constant destructive thoughts in her mind, Amber's physical being reflected her mental and emotional state. Unfortunately for her, she refused to see the negative implications of her life choices and lived in denial to the pain she had caused others. She continues to struggle immensely with her health and looks far older than her fifty-four years of age would suggest.

For Derrick and Amber, the pain they caused others and the pain they continued to cause themselves throughout their lives, was fed by their immense levels of denial which allowed them to blame everyone else in their lives (except themselves) for the negativity and hurt their decisions had resulted in. If they had managed to *accept* their roles in their outcomes in any way, maybe they wouldn't have caused so much pain and damage, both to themselves and to others. Acceptance of who they were as people, would have led them to re-evaluate how they chose to live their lives, and maybe they would have chosen to reappraise their actions and behaviors also.

Some people believe in Karma, or they say "What goes around comes around" or "It's a 'you reap what you sow' world". The reality is that whatever you choose to do in your life, it will one way or another come back to you. If you choose to break the law, the criminal system will punish you. If you choose to break a contract, litigation may result. If you hurt other people in your life, then that hurt will also be felt by you. Many people can't see that the common denominator of bad things happening in their lives is … *themselves*. It is this denial of their realities and the refusal to accept responsibility and accountability that will always perpetuate their outcomes.

Sometimes, it takes Therapy or Counselling to help you see the reality of your situation. The reality could be, the richer your life is the more likely you are to experience pain, loss and emotional upheaval. Why? Because the more things we try to achieve in our lives, the more "failures" we may encounter; the more friends we may have, the more 'goodbyes' there may end up being; the more ideas and goals we have, the more sacrifices we may need to make. If you lead a fuller and richer life, then you will appreciate the opportunities that come your way, *and you will also intuitively know the secret of accepting what you need to accept in your life to enable you to be more fulfilled.*

If you find it difficult to accept things in your life, you could be symbolically withdrawing from participating fully in what you do. By trying not to be a victim in your 'World of Denial', you may ironically end up as a victim of your own fears anyway.

The key is, if you can create a positive experience from anything that is negative about you or your life, it will allow you to find personal meaning and growth, and allow you to create value from *any* experience.

LEARN TO CREATE VALUE OUT OF ANYTHING THAT LIFE HANDS YOU.

You have to understand that life *is* about choices and that you have to always remain conscious of the fact that you have these choices. You choose how you react to a situation. You can't control the external stimuli, but you *can* control how you react to it.

ACCEPTANCE REDUCES YOUR FEARS AND CREATES MEANING TO YOUR LIFE. THIS LEADS TO A GREATER SENSE OF FULFILMENT.

Does acceptance mean that you shouldn't act to change things that go wrong in your life?

Don't confuse acceptance with inertia or apathy. Acceptance means positive action. Denial to your situation means giving up. It is only when you see possibility for change that you can work towards affecting that change. You can say "*No*" to a negative situation as it is, but you can say "*Yes*" to the opportunities and possibilities for growth that it offers. If you believe a situation in your life is desperate and hopeless, then both on a conscious and subconscious level, your behaviour will keep confirming that.

If you believe a situation is not desperate and hopeless, then you become open to the new opportunities to create whatever you choose to in your life. If you choose to believe this and focus on saying "Yes" to your World, then you won't be

215

paralyzed by fear as you go after the possibilities inherent in any given situation.

Acceptance doesn't mean giving up!

ACCEPTANCE MEANS BEING PROACTIVE AND ACTING ON YOUR BELIEF THAT YOU CAN CREATE PURPOSE AND OPPORTUNITY IN WHATEVER SITUATION YOU FIND YOURSELF IN.

This equates to you being able to channel your resources to find positive, constructive and healthy ways to deal with difficult and adverse conditions; It equates to acting on strength and not weakness; It equates to having the understanding that is necessary to survey the many options available to you, and then being able to choose the ones that enhance your growth.

Acceptance means becoming aware of, and alive to all the new possibilities available to you. It *does not* equate to you being apathetic, oblivious to your potential, and then subsequently being helpless and hopeless.

On one level, whereas the idea of acceptance may be fairly easy to comprehend for you, *learning* to accept may require a great deal of awareness. It can be very easy for you to react negatively and be ultra-critical of what happens to you, and in many ways, this may be your 'natural response'- to either end up dismissive or be in denial. It is not always easy to accept extreme sadness and difficulty in your life, such as in the following scenarios: Losing your job; getting injured in an accident; coping with a child that is ill; getting a divorce; suffering bankruptcy; losing a loved one, etc.

Therefore, it is very important that you always bear in mind:

MANY PEOPLE HAVE SUFFERED EXTREME HARDSHIP IN THEIR LIVES, YET THEY HAVE OVERCOME ANY ADVERSITY THAT LIFE HAS DEALT THEM.

The choice really is yours as to whether you choose to see yourself as a victim and a loser, or whether you choose to see yourself as an achiever and a winner. Achieving and winning will leave you with a much greater sense of accomplishment in your life, and this in turn will leave you feeling far more fulfilled with your outcomes.

It is worth every effort to learn how to achieve and how to be a winner. The following steps will help you:

I) Create awareness when/that you are being negative and living in denial over certain situations in your life. You may need to surround yourself with constant positive awareness reminders in the form of notes, stickers, messages on your phone/computer/tablet, positive pictures/posters, fridge magnets, in fact anything that will help you to remain aware on a daily basis. Many a time, we drift off into negativity or denial as a default, and we need to constantly remain conscious and aware of the positives around us.

Look for quotes and sayings that also constantly keep you aware, open minded and appreciative. The following examples may be useful for you:

"Love people for who they are, instead of judging them for who they are not."

"If you don't start appreciating what's right in front of you, you may end up losing it."

"A stumbling block to the pessimist is a stepping stone to the optimist."

"We tend to forget that happiness doesn't come as a result of getting something we don't have, but of appreciating what we *do* have."

"If you wait until you are ready, you will be waiting the rest of your life."

"Behind me is infinite power; before me is endless possibility; around me is boundless opportunity."

"Look at everything as though you were seeing it either for the first or last time."

"There are blessings every day. Find them. Create them. Treasure them."

"Accept no-one's definition of *your* life; define yourself!"

"God gives his hardest battles to his strongest soldiers."

Use quotes and sayings like the ones above on a daily basis to constantly keep you on track in being aware and accepting in your life.

II) Once you have consciousness of what you need to be aware of, you can physically affirm your ideas that help create acceptance. You can do this by simply, *nodding your head*. Whenever you feel that you are actively being aware and accepting of the situations in your life, just nod your head in agreement. There is something acutely powerful in matching your physical actions to your mindful thoughts. It gives you a deeper sense of inner strength that you *will* be able to accomplish what you need to.

III) Remaining on the 'physical action' theme, learn to physically relax your body, starting from the top of your head, down to the tip of your toes. Focus on letting your tensions go whenever you feel tense or anxious. It is extremely underrated with regards to how much the body can take the lead whenever you need to set up more positive feelings, and whenever you need to let go of more negative ones.

IV) Try to find ways whereby you can create *value* from any given situation and experience. Always be mindful and ask yourself these types of questions:

"How can I learn to improve myself as a result of what has happened to me?"

"How can I use this experience in a beneficial and advantageous way for me?"

"What can I possibly learn from this situation and experience?"

Your subconscious mind doesn't judge you, it just works on the premise of what is your chosen reality. If you have the intent to create something positive, then your subconscious will ensure that your outcomes will be positive, and that positivity will be in your reality. As mentioned earlier, let go of trying to predict what the outcome 'should' be, instead, be open for positive opportunities that your mind may be incapable of predicting.

V) Try not to feel so frustrated with yourself when you are immersed in negativity ... just be patient. Although this requires some diligence, it *will* be worthwhile for you. Have a deeper belief that you *will* eventually get bored of being depressed and negative, and that you *will* eventually find a way out of the quagmire. Make a mental note that you *will* find acceptance, happiness, peace and fulfilment at some point.

In life, we can find a way out of whatever predicament we are in, one way or another, if we truly want to. By accepting the situations we find ourselves in, we will find the necessary solutions much quicker, and as a result, the quality of our lives will be vastly improved, both in the short-term and long-term.

VI) Start practicing your levels of awareness on everyday events in your life, not just the major ones. This will create an 'awareness mindset' for you, whereby, by practicing on not so important events, this will result in you automatically thinking the same way when addressing more important situations. For example, if your train is delayed, or your bus is taking too long, or you are stuck in a traffic jam, then focus on your predicament and accept your situation. Be positive, find something alternative and fulfilling to do: read, send texts, make a call, do some work, or do *anything* else that will take your mind off the negativity and possible anger a situation like this may create for you. Sometimes the key to acceptance involves not only awareness, but also distraction techniques to help you cope in a difficult situation. Once you develop these behavioral patterns, then when something more serious happens to you, it will become 'second nature' for you in being able to deal with the more difficult and serious situations that may arise.

It is important to be mindful of your behaviour in the situations that you find yourself in – Sometimes there is absolutely nothing that you can do about them, therefore it is advisable to try and make the best of whatever the experience.

For example, if you are waiting for someone, or keeping someone else waiting for you, try to be more aware of your thoughts so you don't get angry or irritable, and then try to use the extra time more wisely. Just call or text who you need to and don't stress over something that is out of your control.

For drivers, 'road rage' is a common expression for getting angry whilst you are driving. If you think about it logically, you won't get anywhere faster by shouting and screaming at other drivers. The only thing that will happen is that your blood pressure will increase as will your stress levels, and the traffic will still be as bad as before. Just listen to the radio or do something else that will take your mind off driving. After all, where is it that you are going to that is *so* important? Another ten or fifteen minutes on your journey will make no difference. As suggested, a phone call ahead should take the pressure off.

Whenever you find yourself getting angry at external stimuli, keep calm, accept what is happening, and remember: ***'Learn to create value out of anything that life hands you'***. That way, you deal with what is happening to you at that precise moment, and you are not resisting your environment. Your life will become less stressed because you will be better able to control yourself and as an added bonus, all your relationships will also improve and develop dramatically. When anything goes wrong for you, it will invariably still teach you something: leave earlier; never choose that restaurant again; don't continually rely on others; be more independent; invest more wisely; end a relationship sooner if the 'danger signals' are there; next time don't get drunk; don't expect favors to be returned … in fact the list is endless. Whatever has or can go wrong for you, will provide you with life lessons and an opportunity to grow and develop if you choose to see it that way.

As mentioned, once you can deal with day-to-day situations, you will be able to handle the more challenging and serious issues that you will have to face in your life. By being aware and accepting, you will notice your levels of fear and denial dissipating as they will be replaced by a greater sense of trust in your ability to handle your environment. As you start to see opportunities and possibilities in your World, you will be able to find purpose and reason in everything that you encounter, *if* you open your mind to that possibility.

In fact, the only times in your life that you will feel angst, fear and trepidation, are when you choose to live in denial and resist what is happening to you. You need to consciously accept what is happening in your life. Learn to let go of stressful/draining situations and people, and stop fighting worthless battles. The key is learning how to view your life so you get the most optimal and beneficial results for yourself.

AWARENESS > ACCEPTANCE > INNER PEACE > FULFILMENT

<u>Summary</u>

<u>Steps to Acceptance:</u>

I) Create awareness whereby you can accept what is happening to you.

II) Create physical affirmation. Say yes and nod your head.

III) Learn to relax physically as well as mentally.

IV) Realign your thinking patterns to: "What can I learn from this experience/situation?"

V) Learn to be more patient. It may take time learning to be more aware and accepting, so don't be too hard on yourself.

VI) Practice your thinking on everyday events until awareness and acceptance become second nature for you.

VII) Learn the concept of acceptance by firstly learning to accept yourself. Say 'yes' to who you are and *accept yourself above all else*, as this is the key to true satisfaction and deeper fulfilment throughout your life.

CHAPTER TEN:

KISMET AND THE POWER OF GIVING

"Things turn out best for those who make the best of the way things turn out."

John Wooden

Would you say that there's a reason for the way things turn out the way they do in your life? Does whatever that happens to you follow a plan you have created for yourself, or does it seem to be more of a set of random events that you react to? Do you always get back what you give out, and are you truly grateful for what you receive in your life? Most of us in relationships or families just 'plod along' and never really question our interactions and relationships... They seem to have a pattern which we have somehow created, and which we follow without ever really questioning why. We never truly appreciate what happens to us and the reasons behind it, and many a time, we even take things and people for granted. When was the last time you were truly grateful and appreciative of the people that mean the most to you in your life? We generally see ourselves as 'loving' and 'giving' but in reality, most of our relationships can be defined as an exchange of sorts, such as, "you do this for me, and I'll do this for you in return". We may not *consciously* think of our behaviour as being so, but the subconscious definitions of our relationships may be exactly like this.

Maybe you automatically carry on your daily existence without questioning or thinking about how and why things are as they are in your life. For example, how grateful are you *really* for the people in your life? Could you easily thank them for the contribution they make to your existence? Why are you with your partner? Should he/she feel lucky that they are with you? What is the true reality of your relationship? Maybe if you are being honest with yourself, you will know that deep down, your partner provides you with a number of advantages:

- Security (both emotional and financial)

- Companionship

- Love

- Nurture

- A sense of not being alone

Do we get this because of pure chance/luck? Is it something to do with fate/kismet? Or do we have to work hard at getting all these benefits?

Most of us operate on some kind of 'hidden barter system', whereby we never truly give anything away unless we get something in return; be it love, money, companionship, appreciation or whatever else it may be. After all, we tend to get back what we give out, but have you ever *genuinely* given something without expecting anything in return?

IF ALL YOUR GIVING IS BASED ON RECEIVING, THEN IMAGINE HOW FEARFUL YOUR EXISTENCE WILL BE.

At some point if you carry on thinking like this, then all your thoughts will naturally develop to, "Well, I am giving out a lot, but am I getting back *enough* from other people?" If you think like this, then at some point, you will try to control both yourself *and* other people. You will control what you give out, and at the same time you will feel the need to control others so that you don't feel used and short-changed; this will eventually create anger, resentment and will destroy your peace of mind. Remember it was said in 'Acts 20:35' that "It is more blessed to give than to receive ..." After all:

GENUINE GIVING TO OTHERS MAKES YOU FEEL BETTER AS A PERSON AND IS AN ALTRUISTIC ACT!

Sometimes though, giving may not always be based on altruism, but may be based on a deeper psychological need to always feel wanted and needed by others. There is a big difference between the two:

* Coleen was from a large family and was always involved in everything they did. Throughout her life, she was very close to her brothers and sisters, and played a central role in family life. When she had her own children and grandchildren, she wanted to be the best mother and grandmother she possibly could. Coleen did everything for her children and grandchildren from washing their clothes to cooking and cleaning after them. From the outside, she was an extremely caring and giving person, always doing her best to provide for her family. The problem was that Coleen couldn't see that *her need* to be needed by others was contributing to her compulsive behaviors. She found it very difficult not to be overly involved in her children's and grandchildren's lives, and she struggled to let them have any independence. Her constant giving was based on a deeper psychological need to be loved and accepted, but what she couldn't see, was that by

her doing everything for everyone, it was a method to have control and to be domineering in her children's and grandchildren's lives. This constant 'doing' and 'giving' was her way of 'bartering'- by *giving*, she wanted back love, appreciation and a continued bond in everyone's lives. The problem for her was that she could never see the value of teaching someone to be self-sufficient and self-reliant. By teaching others to be that, then maybe they wouldn't need her as much anymore. So rather than 'teach', she continued to 'give'.

This kind of giving is flawed, because although most parents feel they are providing care, love and nurture for their children, they overlook the fundamental importance of teaching their children valuable skills to cope with the demands of life. In most societies and ethnic groups, children don't always become fully developed adults because they struggle without the necessary skills needed to grow and develop in the right way.

Although most adults think they are good at just giving without expecting anything in return, the reality is that they are *not*. So why do we find it so difficult to just give altruistically? Evidence points to two major components:

I) Giving without expecting in return, is an acquired skill which many of us have never truly learned or mastered.

II) Giving requires us to be mature adults, but the problem is that just like children, we would rather receive "presents" than buy them, so in that sense, we never truly grow up.

These skills are intertwined, and require us to be both mindful and to be able to practice them. The reason we never really practice them is because we can't see when we are being childish or when we aren't truly giving to others. We always seem to expect something rather than give something, so in many ways, we are just deceiving ourselves to the reality of our behaviour. Although we may *appear* to be adults, if we are honest, our child-like needs and behaviors dominate our thought processes and cloud our judgments and reactions.

Learning how to give is a very important life-lesson. Once we learn how to give without expectation, then we become more rounded as adults. In fact, if you think about it, being needy is an innate characteristic that we all have – when we are born we just want to be cared for and nurtured, whatever time of day or night we want attention or food, we then cry until we get it. The belief is that as we grow, we become more and more independent and self-reliant. Although as we grow, and can take care of ourselves more and more until we reach adulthood, that innate neediness we are all born with, can still be a part of us. As adults, we are still fearful that our basic needs (shelter, food, security, friendship, intimacy and family) will not be met. Even if they are met, we are fearful it is only for a temporary time or that we may lose them altogether. This way of thinking presents us with continual dilemmas and turmoil – if we are so fearful of losing what we already have, then how can we give? We therefore, either wittingly or unwittingly, become very manipulative and selfish as we try to constantly get everything that we need, mostly because of our innate instinct for survival. These negative behaviors will then manifest themselves as negative emotions such as feeling angry, dissatisfied, fearful, frustrated, helpless, mistrustful, trapped, and unfulfilled. As a result, it becomes difficult for us to support the well-being of other people if their needs in any way conflict with our own needs.

As we have an element of fear that permeates our lives from young to old, the idea that our wellbeing can depend on others can be a frightening concept. As a child our fears are based on who will take care of us and look after us, and ironically as adults, those fears never really go away. As adults our fear of loss also revolves around our partners, friends, children, and of course our parents. The problem with this inherent fear is that, if we live our lives being scared, we can never truly give to others, because we always *need* and *want*.

If you live in fear, your world is filled with scarcity instead of abundance. You will be too scared to 'give anything away'; your modus operandi is to take and not to give. Your world is always half empty: There is not enough love; Not enough positive attention; Not enough praise; Not enough joy; Not enough money. In fact if you live in fear, your world will always be scarce with not enough of anything. If you genuinely feel that your life lacks something in one area, you subconsciously then become very protective in many other areas of your life. If you are fearful, then this can manifest itself in different behaviors patterns, such as:

- Jealous people who try to hold on to their partners and fear their independence.

- People who remain 'closed', worried that others will steal their ideas or skills.

- High maintenance people who demand so much from their partners, that they will either end up alone or with inappropriate 'enablers'.

- Married people who constantly blame their spouses or children from holding them back in life.

- Successful business people who are always desperate to seek the approval of their peers.

- Corporate executives who make uncalculated and irresponsible business decisions that could affect the lives of many other people.

This is just a cross-section of people who are living their lives in fear, and are too frightened to 'give' in case it affects their own survival. In many ways, we are all afflicted by fear, the question is "How debilitating is it in your life?" Also, "To what level does it stop you from fully participating in your life?" In reality, we all *think* that we are good at giving, but the truth is, we are all very good at taking because we haven't truly been taught how to give. We are all told that the world is a dangerous place, and that we have to be wary of people. We are careful that we don't get tricked or taken advantage of. Our mindset is that we shouldn't do anything unless we get something back, and if we don't get anything back, then we are being used. Of course, we *do* need to be careful about many things, after all, survival *is* innate, but we shouldn't be blinded by fear in all our interactions. Again remember that 'Balance is the Key'.

Think about the following concept:

WHEN YOU GIVE ALTRUISTICALLY INSTEAD OF EXPECTING SOMETHING BACK, THEN PARADOXICALLY MORE WILL COME BACK TO YOU THAN YOU COULD HAVE POSSIBLY IMAGINED.

You need to drop your levels of expectation from other people, because when you learn to do that, your happiness is in your hands and not in the hands of others. Expectation leads to large levels of disappointment, as well as feelings of not being treated as you should be by others.

NO EXPECTATION = HIGHER LEVELS OF SELF-SATISFACTION AND SELF-RELIANCE.

(When discussing expectation in this context, it relates to expecting from other people, it doesn't relate to you setting yourself high standards and then doing your utmost to attain them {'Personal Expectation'}. When it comes to achievements for *yourself* then of course it is natural to expect yourself to accomplish what you set out to do.)

The importance of understanding this concept is immense, otherwise you will continue to perpetuate your feelings of scarcity, and nothing you ever do or obtain will ever be enough for you. You become like a bottomless-pit, just wanting more and more, with no satisfaction ever in sight. Attention is never enough; love is never enough; money is never enough: praise is never enough. In fact, without true satisfaction, you feel as though there is a void in your life that can never be filled. The deeper psychological issue here is that you live in a constant state of fear, whereby you worry that you will lose what you have, and that eventually, you will have nothing left. With this mindset, you hang on to what you have for dear life, and the concept of 'sharing and giving' doesn't even enter your mind. This can of course lead on to another 'self-fulfilling prophecy'. If you see yourself as losing out and ending up with nothing, then your subconscious sees that also, and that may become your reality. In other words:

YOU ATTRACT WHAT YOU FEAR MOST

If this is how you behave or if this is how you see your life, then you need to change your ways. To stop yourself from fearing 'having a lack of something' and 'scarcity' in your life, you need to do the *opposite* of what you have been doing up until now. If your existence has been based on selfishness, or being self-absorbed in any way; If life for you has meant taking what you can instead of giving back something; Or, if your life has equated to individual profit at the expense of others, then surely for you, it is time to leave a more positive legacy of who you are and what your values represent. Instead of hanging onto everything for dear life, learn to let go, give some things away, and release things to give you a greater sense of freedom. The strange thing about life is that the more we desperately hold onto something, the more likely we are to lose it. It's weird how life works in that way, but unfortunately it does – the more you hold onto your partner, the more you hold onto money, the more you hold onto your job, the more you hold onto *anything*, then the more likely you are to lose it. You may think you should give when you are 'rich', or when you feel you have an abundance, but the thing is, you only ever feel that way once you have given, and not before!

GIVING > FEELING ABUNDANT AND BEING ABUNDANT

It may be difficult for you to grasp this ideology, but by being more relaxed and altruistic, you feel a greater sense of power and a greater sense of control in your life as you become less suspicious of people and more willing to share and give what you have. Also, once your fears start to disappear, you begin to feel more 'adult' about your behaviour and who you are, instead of living in a world of child-like angst, fear and worry. Bear in mind, *your ultimate goal is to be a well-rounded and balanced adult who doesn't live in constant fear of losing everything*.

<u>**What should you give and how should you do it?**</u>

<u>**Give Love**</u>

This is probably the most important thing. It is a small word with an incredibly large meaning in every area of our lives. Love between partners; love between parent and child; love between siblings; love between us and anything else that can evoke powerful emotions in us. The danger for us is that love can be an incredibly selfish and self-centered emotion. It can be very difficult for us to share what we love with others. Sometimes love can bring about other strong but debilitating emotions such as: being overly controlling and possessive; being jealous; being fearful and worried … In fact, when it comes to love, you need to be very strong and understanding with the emotions you are dealing with. For example, novices of romantic love may display all the negative traits mentioned above, before they learn to be more trusting of themselves and others. After all, very few people have not made mistakes when it comes to affairs of the heart.

Giving your Love means:

- Allowing someone to work out who they are and giving them the space and support they need to be able to do that.

- Allowing someone to learn and grow without feeling fearful, threatened or worried.

- Allowing someone to handle his/her life and then acting appropriately to the choices and decisions that they make.

− Allowing someone to be who they are without trying to influence, manipulate or change them.

Many relationships don't have any of the above. These relationships can be said to be based on control, jealousy, personal gain, or neediness. Real love and balanced love *must* equate to your ability to give …

"Immature love says: 'I love you because I *need* you.'

Mature love says: 'I need you because I *love* you.'"

Erich Fromm

Another healthy way to look at relationships and the concept of love can be expressed by this quote:

"Being deeply loved by someone gives you strength, while loving someone deeply gives you courage."

Lao Tzu

By truly loving someone and giving unconditionally, we lose our fears and in return gain courage and maturity. Surely the gains are far too great to ignore.

Give Gratitude

Being thankful and grateful for what you have and for the people in your life should be easy to do, but the reality is, that it can be difficult to appreciate fully what you have. Many a time, we actually take things for granted and this can also lead us to losing the things we love and cherish the most.

Expressing gratitude just means being able to say "Thank You" to your world. Always bear in mind that both you and your show of gratitude mean something, both to yourself, and to other people. Never underestimate the power that being grateful has. Always thank the people who have given you something in your life, however large or trivial you may deem it to be. If this seems a difficult thing for you to do, then start with everyday situations such as thanking your partner, thanking your work colleagues, and thanking people you encounter for their help or services. Let gratitude become your mindset and let your "Thank Yous" enter your consciousness, so they become a part of your daily thinking. At first it may be difficult to say "Thank You" to everyone and everything around you, but with time and practice, and by showing gratitude for what you have, eventually you will feel more at peace with your life and also feel much more satisfied with everything.

How should you start to show gratitude in your life?

Think of everyone who is presently in your life and also people from your past who have contributed significantly to your life in any way (include everyone who has contributed, both in a positive and negative way).

Make a list of their names (either on a piece of paper or your phone/tablet/PC etc.). Then next to their names, write down everything they have done for you and how they have added to your life. Remember, even from any negative encounters, some positives did result as you learned something from that person and experience. Look for the lessons you learned, even if you felt you were hard-done-by or mistreated at the time. Once you have created a list of people and all their contributions to your life, then systematically show each and every person gratitude for enhancing your life in some way. It is important you acknowledge every person who has contributed to your life, even if that person has caused you anger, bitterness and resentment (you may in fact still feel that way towards them).

If someone from your past has hurt you, then focus hard to truly forgive them. By forgiving them, you take away the power that they still hold over you. Once your negativity has left, then thank them for the life-lesson they gave you. Of course this will be very difficult because we may still want people to suffer for what they have done to us. But by carrying around that kind of negativity with you, you will *continue* to be the victim. Forgive them, because "The best revenge is living well!" If you learn to forgive people who have hurt you, you also take a step towards accepting responsibility for whatever role you played in that experience. By healing any negative relationships within yourself, it will also have the added bonus of contributing positively to your physical and emotional health and well-being.

If you continue to hold negative feelings about people from your past, those *past* feelings also become part of your *present* thinking. You relive those emotions and experiences *in the now*; In fact they always remain with you. You carry the negativity from your past into your present, literally like carrying 'emotional baggage' on your journey through life. You need to get rid of past feelings of anger, pain and resentment, before you can let love and gratitude become a part of who you are now.

"Develop an attitude of gratitude and give thanks for everything that happens to you, knowing that every step forward is a step toward achieving something bigger and better than your current situation."

Brian Tracy

Another good way to view gratitude is also expressed in the following quote:

"Gratitude unlocks the fullness of life. It turns what we have into enough, chaos to order, confusion to clarity. It can turn a meal into a feast, a house into a home, a stranger into a friend."

Melody Beattie

Give Praise

The strange thing about our minds and patterns of thinking, is that it is *so* easy to be negative and critical, but it is *so* difficult to express our appreciation and to praise people. In fact, the closer the person is, the more difficult we usually find it to praise them. If we have any negativity in our thoughts, such as anger, bitterness or resentment, then praising our partners, friends, children, colleagues, or even our parents, can be very difficult. If we can overlook any of the negativity that we hold on to, and let go of it, we open the door to be more positive towards our nearest and dearest, and at the same time we allow those positive feelings to be reciprocated.

We want and sometimes *expect* our loved ones to be caring and supportive of us in what we do. However, as already mentioned, it is so easy for us to be negative and critical, especially of our partners, and the reality is that we are not always as appreciative of them as we think we are. Of course it is important for us to have friends and family who are caring, loving and supportive of us, but we need to remember that we have to always give praise and be appreciative of *them* at all times also.

BECOME WHAT YOU WISH TO ATTRACT AND BE THE TYPE OF PERSON THAT YOU WOULD LIKE TO MEET AND BE WITH!

Giving compliments and praise should come naturally for you, and should be given with no ulterior motives. In this meaning, it refers to you giving praise without looking to be praised back, or complimenting someone without 'fishing' for compliments yourself. You shouldn't compliment and praise people in the hope that they will like you, and on the same token, you shouldn't just keep giving and giving if you feel you are being used by someone. By giving, there really should be no other meaning behind it, other than *you want to give in order to make someone else happy*!

Give Help

Again, it is strange that if we feel we have struggled for something in life, or have suffered some hardship along the way, we then have the tendency to hold onto what we have learned, and become the 'gatekeeper' to our experiences and knowledge. In some way, we want to see others struggle as much as we had to and we aren't especially forthcoming in helping others to succeed. This can particularly be the case if we are 'competitive' or if we feel threatened by other people, such as in the work place for example. We withhold information or help that could promote growth in other people.

The problem for you if you are like this, is that, at some point in the future you may need the help of others and then "the favour" will be returned back to you, or you may even miss out on a possible friendship because the person you could have helped, would have reciprocated your act of kindness. On a professional level, you could also miss out on a possible support system. You should give and be as helpful as possible, and do it without expectation. Again, the ironic thing here is that, what you give out will come back to you tenfold, one way or another.

When you choose to withhold your help, you are doing so on the grounds of negativity: fear, mistrust, suspicion, etc. When you help other people, it is because you believe and trust in yourself, as well as in your environment. You have to change your mindset if you are a naturally closed and unhelpful person. Understand that by helping others, your influence on the world is greatly magnified and that people will respect you more and be thankful for your generosity … In other words, you literally *do* become a bigger person in the eyes of other people.

"No-one is useless in this world who lightens the burdens of another."

Charles Dickens

Another helpful quote to bear in mind:

"The best antidote I know for worry is work. The best cure for weariness is the challenge of helping someone who is even more tired. One of the great ironies of life is this: he or she who serves almost always benefits *more* than he or she who is served."

Gordon B. Hinckley

Give Hope

When you brighten someone else's dark existence by being their beacon of hope, you not only help that person, but you also help yourself. Many people work in caring professions because the rewards are far greater than monetary value alone. A large part of caring for others, involves providing them with hope; Hope that everything will eventually get better. This is the premise that keeps doctors, nurses, health care professionals, psychologists, charities, etc. continuing to do what they do.

BY HELPING AND CARING, YOU PROVIDE HOPE

The same can be said for you in your life. Be the person who helps others and leads the way for people, be the shining light that illuminates the lives of everyone that you know or meet. Help them to have dreams, goals and hopes for their future, because by doing this, you also grow as a person and become more content and satisfied in *your* life. One of the biggest reasons people feel so apathetic in their lives, is because they feel helpless and hopeless, they can't really see a way forwards in their lives. If you can be the person who your family, friends and colleagues look to for guidance and hope, the rewards for you too will be immeasurable. Having hope is one of the most important ingredients to live a contented, happy and joyous life, in fact, if you have hope that everything will turn out well for you, it will provide you with the strength you need to carry on doing what you need to do in your day-to-day activities.

"They say a person needs just three things to be truly happy in this world: someone to love, something to do, and something to *hope* for."

Tom Bodett

Give Time

It is said that "Time is an Abstract Concept", but the reality is that for us in our lives, it is a finite commodity and a very valuable one also because we never seem to have enough of it! It is the one thing you can never get back or replace- you can replace a partner, you can replace a job, you can get back money that you have lost, but you can *never* get back or replace lost time! Therefore use your time wisely. If you truly want to be more *caring, loving and nurturing* in your life, then give some of your valuable time away by helping people with their problems either in a proactive way, or just by listening (this is a good start). You can also volunteer to help children, the elderly or the underprivileged in your community. If you give your time to help out anyone who may need it, do it with a sense of pride and joy, rather than doing it with a sense of obligation (many people *appear* to be altruistic and helping by giving up their time, but they are doing it primarily for *themselves*, not for the good of others). If you can do something for other people in this world, then it will really leave you with a sense of *counting for something or someone*. If your time and efforts change the lives of other people, then *of course* you count!

The positive effects of giving your time and feeling as though you count are two-fold. Primarily you are doing it for the benefit of other people, but the energy and strength you get from making an effort 'to be there' for others, is striking. Not only do you become a better person, but you enrich the lives of everyone else around you also.

"When we love, we always strive to become better than we are. When we strive to become better than we are, everything around us becomes better too."

Paulo Coelho

Give Money

For many people, money is a taboo subject. We never really discuss it with other people, because in many ways, it has been used as a benchmark to gauge success. Even if you are *rich* in every other area of your life, if you don't have as much money as you would like, you see yourself as some sort of failure (or worse still, you think *other people* see you as a failure). On the other hand, if you have made lots of money, yet *every* other area of your life is floundering, then you are still viewed as affluent and successful. So in many ways, it is natural that most of us don't want to discuss money, because in reality, we don't want to be judged too harshly, both by others and by *ourselves*. It is also a subject that we never really learn about, we don't learn about it formally, it is knowledge that we acquire 'along the way'. Some of us get lucky in acquiring both knowledge and money, while others have looked at money as a subject in itself to be actively learned about. Others still are not 'good with money' and life has and always will be a struggle.

Yet however 'good' or 'bad' we are with money, most of us are fearful of not getting enough, or losing what we have. Regardless of how much money we have, the fear of ending up *penniless* is very real for some of us. This can manifest itself in two ways:-

a) You become extremely frugal and try to hold on to what you have and don't spend money on anything, so for you, "enough" will never really be enough.

241

b) You may develop a carefree attitude and not take too much care over your spending, whereby you spend what you have on unimportant things, so paradoxically you don't have any money left to worry about (even though deep down you actually do worry about your finances).

It may be beneficial for you to actually *learn* more about money. There are many websites that provide you with comparisons and information regarding investments, loans, savings, making claims, and so forth. Ignorance really is no excuse in today's world. You can learn more about having better control and understanding of your finances. Information really is power in this instance: the power to release you from your fears.

Once you are less fearful and you can 'loosen up', you will be able to spend or give away money with a greater peace of mind. If you are holding on tightly to what you have, for you, the world is filled with scarcity. If you can *enjoy* your money, then for you, the world is abundant. Above all, as previously pointed out, ***Balance is the Key***.

"Money has never made man happy, nor will it, there is nothing in its nature to produce happiness. The more of it one has, the more one wants."

Benjamin Franklin

"Many people take no care of their money till they come nearly to the end of it, and others do just the same with their time."

Johann Wolfgang von Goethe

There are many other things that you can also give of course, but the overall idea of giving, is to create contentment, fulfilment and above all, abundance in your world. Giving is about allowing things to flow naturally around you and through you and it's about not resisting 'the flow of nature'. In many ways, you can view it as this:

GIVING IS ALL ABOUT OUTFLOW

In many ways, your life is already filled with contentment and abundance, but you probably haven't noticed it or 'tuned into it'. Understanding and appreciating what you have, is also a skill that you may need to practice. The best way to practice this, is to literally *write down* ALL the positive things that are in your life, or have been in your life. However large or small you deem the positive act to be, write it down, so you can always see that your life has had, and continues to have many positives to it. Write down a minimum of at least one hundred things, and then try to keep adding to your list. The problem for most of us is that we have no trouble remembering all the negative episodes in our lives, but for some reason, we quickly forget all the positive experiences that we have lived through. If you actually make an effort to find the blessings that are in your life, you will then be able to focus on them. They are all around you and have been so throughout your life. Whether you choose to see them or not, is up to you. Again it's a choice:

DO YOU CHOOSE TO SEE THE ABUNDANCE IN YOUR LIFE, OR DO YOU CHOOSE TO LOOK FOR THE SCARCITY?

Scarcity and lacking doesn't relate to money or possessions, it relates to love. Love is actually the one thing that you have total control over and create an abundance of it *anytime* if you choose to. Remain vigilant in your efforts to be a better person: a person who cares, a person who loves, and above all a person who *gives*. Your objective should be to understand that you can contribute to your surroundings, you *can* be a giver, but before you can give, you have to understand that you actually *do* have something to give.

GIVING > FEELINGS OF POWER AND LOVE = FEARING NOTHING

Stop being a 'taker' in life and figure out how to be a giver. By giving you lose your fears because you realise that *'The power is in your hands*; *you are not dependent on anyone else for your happiness or survival'.*

"We make a living by what we get. We make a life by what we give."

Winston Churchill

<u>KISMET</u>

Many people believe that they may not be in full control of their lives, that there may be some other power or outside force that determines what happens to them. Of course, as we have looked at, outside factors, attraction, how we react and what *we choose* to do can all determine how our lives pan out. If you believe that your life has a 'pre-ordained destiny' that is out of your control, then the danger for you may be that you don't take full responsibility for your life and its outcomes. You may believe that kismet/fate plays a part in what happens to you. In life, of course many random things may happen from which your life can take on a totally different direction or course of events. We randomly meet people who become important to us: our partners, friends, job connections, etc., but what we choose to do with these random meetings is totally in *our* control. **You can say that *kismet* provides you**

with the tools, but what you choose to build with those tools is in *your* control.

Definition of Kismet

The word 'kismet' derives from the Middle-East and is used in both Arabic and Turkish. Its literal meaning is 'portion, division or lot' and when used, implies that you have your lot in life, or your *fate*. People in the region use it in the sense that "If it's meant to be, it will happen." It is also used in relation to something significant that comes about entirely by chance. For example, randomly meeting a person who ends up being your husband or wife = kismet.

When you encounter something by chance that seems like 'it was meant to be', then you could view it as kismet (your destiny/your fate).

It is a development of events beyond your control and it could be said that it's determined by a 'supernatural power', whereby things are destined to happen, turn out, or act in a particular way.

"Sometimes the slightest things change the directions of our lives, the merest breath of a circumstance, a random moment that connects like a meteorite striking the Earth. Lives have swiveled and changed direction on the strength of a chance remark."

Bryce Courtenay

The question is, 'How do you view your existence'? As already asked, do you see it as following a plan that you have created for yourself, or does it seem to be more of a set of random events that you react to? The truth is that life is a combination of things that happen to you, both planned and random.

Always bear in mind that:

KISMET PRESENTS YOU WITH THE OPPORTUNITY, BUT IT IS *YOU* WHO DETERMINES WHAT THE OUTCOME IS.

"There is so much about my fate that I cannot control, but other things do fall under the jurisdiction. I can decide how I spend my time, whom I interact with, whom I share my body and life and money and energy with. I can select what I can read and eat and study. I can choose how I'm going to regard unfortunate circumstances in my life- whether I will see them as curses or opportunities. I can choose my words and the tone of voice in which I speak to others. And most of all, I can choose my thoughts."

Elizabeth Gilbert

Be in control of your life:

"It matters not how strait the gate, how charged with punishments the scroll, I am the Master of my fate: I am the Captain of my soul."

William Ernest Henley

CHAPTER ELEVEN:

YOUR HIGHER CONSCIOUS AND THE LAW OF ATTRACTION

"When you concentrate your energy purposely on the future possibility that you aspire to realise, your energy is passed on to it and makes it attracted to you with a force stronger than the one you directed towards it."

Stephen Richards

So far, we have looked at many examples, techniques and powerful tools, such as: taking full responsibility for your actions and behaviour; focusing on making the right choices; understanding appreciation and gratitude; learning to accept your environment; the art of positive thinking; understanding your role in decision making, and so forth. Once you learn to master these various powerful tools, and learn to implement them in your daily life, you will start to notice that your deeper feelings of fulfilment and satisfaction will increase no end.

The reason for this is because you are creating a new pattern for yourself whereby you are then tapping into a deeper consciousness of yourself and how you operate and think. This deeper awareness and understanding of yourself can also be termed as your "Higher Conscious". Also, this deeper understanding of who you are creates a new plane of existence for you which surpasses your 'everyday level' of difficulty, strife and struggle. Your "Higher Conscious" implies a transcendence of that part of you which is stuck on the petty things in your life which often lead to feelings of fear, negativity, scarcity and worry.

In many psychological schools of thought, this Higher Conscious is capable of a high degree of attraction, attunement and sensitivity to a harmonious existence for us. Many of your more admirable virtues such as aspiration, caring, creativity, empathy, inspiration, intuition, joy, love, sympathy and trust, can all be contributed to your Higher Conscious thinking patterns. In many ways, this is the *essence* of who you really are. When you reach this level, your attention is enhanced, improved and much more refined, and other aspects of your mind such as thought and perception are transcended beyond the automatic thoughts of hum-drum everyday existence. In other words, you achieve *a greater sense of reality*. Many a time, we are just living a 'reactive existence', whereby we just react to the world around us, without truly participating or being conscious of what is happening and who we are.

You have great potential within yourself, but this usually remains inchoate because your everyday existence involves automatic, mechanical and neurotic modes of behaviour which drain you of your energy and therefore leave you with no room for personal or spiritual development. In a deeper psychological sense, you then begin to 'project' your occurrences onto the external stimuli you encounter. In other words, whatever occurs in your life, you blame your sufferings on outer circumstances or on other individuals.

Your Higher Conscious enables you to understand that any alienation, suffering or upset in your life, are your own responsibility and is dependent on your mind's acceptance (acquiescence).

It could be said that your Higher Conscious is based on all your admirable virtues and also on your ability to understand your role in any suffering that occurs in your life.

In life, many of us seem to be searching for something that could make our lives complete, but in reality, we don't really know what we are searching for. No matter what we seem to do or have, we still feel alienated, empty and lonely, and nothing seems capable of making us feel fulfilled and satisfied. Having these negative feelings often leads us to search desperately for something to 'fill the void'. We often think something 'new' will solve the problem: new clothes, a new job, a new house, a new car, a new partner even. Advertisers know how we work on a psychological level, so a lot of advertising is geared towards our inadequacies and feelings of *un*-fulfilment. That is why there is no shortage of 'Retail Therapy': dating sites, consumer goods, shopping centres, car manufacturers, estate agents, etc., etc., all with the aim of helping us 'fill the void' that we have, and at the same time helping us part with our hard earned money. Be honest, do you really need half the things that you buy? Have you ever stopped to wonder *why* you buy the things you do?

The reality is that something new doesn't satiate the inadequacies of old.

Maybe what you are really looking for in your life is learning how to align yourself with your Higher Conscious. When you feel such a sense of emptiness or loss in your life, then it is natural you try to fill those feelings with something, be it consumer goods, be it food, be it religion or be it an ideology. As human beings, we all look to cure our feelings of emptiness and loss with *something*, the question is, how detrimental is that *something* to us in the long-term. Maybe aligning yourself with your Higher Conscious means finding "the essence of who you are" within yourself. So you don't need to have or use anything externally to find the answers that you're looking for internally.

In our lives today, although there is a lot more emphasis on improving ourselves in every way, from body to mind and to spirit, we still primarily concern ourselves with our body and mind. Our appearance has become more and more important to us. Our understanding of ourselves is getting better and better with the help of technology, media and professionals in the areas of counselling and psychology. Yet somehow, our spiritual sides as human beings are still being neglected. In terms of spirituality, it doesn't necessarily relate in any way to religion, but more to our human spirit. Most people are not aware they have a spiritual side, and often confuse the concept with the meaning in the religious sense.

Understand that you need to tap into your spiritual side to help you rid yourself of perpetual discontentment. Remember, your Higher Conscious is where your *admirable virtues* can be found. It is where your *true qualities* are.

You may have been in touch with your Higher Conscious and not even have known it. Let us look at some of your admirable virtues in example form:

Aspiration – Have you ever created dreams and goals for yourself and then done your utmost to accomplish them?

Caring – Have you ever looked after or provided for the needs of others, irrespective of how you felt about it?

Creativity – Have you ever involved the use of your imagination in order to create something beautiful?

Empathy – Have you ever felt someone else's pain to the point where you ended up crying?

Inspiration – Have you ever felt the urge to do something, or helped someone else by inspiring them to achieve something?

Intuition – Have you ever understood or known something immediately without thought or reasoning?

Joy – Have you ever felt overwhelmed at the beauty of nature and been filled with a sense of awe and abundance?

Love – Have you ever loved someone so much, that *their* happiness meant more to you than *your own happiness* did?

Sympathy – Have you ever 'been there' for someone when they truly needed you, irrespective of how *you* were feeling at the time?

Trust – Have you ever put your happiness into someone else's hands 100%?

If you have done any of these things, it could be said you were operating from your Higher Conscious. You transcended your automatic every day existence in order to help others or to look within yourself to find a higher level of being, one that involved, dreams, beauty and love.

If your Higher Conscious is in tune with your partner's, then together your relationship and your life will be filled with a phenomenal sense of power and love. The key is to help each other grow in your relationship so that you both develop your *admirable virtues*, your *true qualities* and your *feelings of happiness* together.

This sense of power can be generated in two ways:

By doing *Good* or by doing *Evil*.

When you operate from a place of doing Evil (and/or Bad things), although you may perceive a sense of power in some way, power from a negative place will never alleviate feelings of alienation, emptiness and loss. In fact, eventually it will just create more fear and mistrust in your life. When you operate from your Higher Conscious, you naturally create feelings of strength, empowerment and plenitude. These positive feelings provide a true sense of power where you dispel all your negative fears and worries.

So in reality, Good will always supersede Evil in one way or another.

It is also the sense of power that stems from your Higher Conscious that can create extraordinary feats of physical or emotional strength in you. Sometimes you may encounter a situation whereby you may deem it to be truly impossible for you to accomplish your goal, either in a physical or emotional sense. Yet, somehow you manage to accomplish it.

This sense of power is also responsible for helping you choose your experiences of life:

When your negative thought processes kick-in these are governed by your negative internal dialogues which we looked at earlier. This negativity is a very selfish part of us and governs all our self-centered desires, needs and wants. Your Subconscious Mind will receive messages from your Conscious Mind which will either be sent via your Higher Conscious or via your Negative Internal Voice (Lower Conscious). You can train yourself to choose from either source.

Your Subconscious Mind is where you store lots of facts and information. It files, sorts and finds information such as names, addresses, numbers, dates, events, etc., etc. Think of your subconscious as your *logical* mind. The Subconscious Mind does not judge or question anything, it does not know right from wrong or what is healthy for us or unhealthy for us. The Subconscious Mind takes its orders from the Conscious Mind and also believes whatever the Conscious Mind tells it, whether it's true or not, or whether it is believable or not.

Your Conscious Mind then has a choice of whether to listen to your Higher Conscious (packed with abundance, love, nurture and positivity) or your Negative Internal Voice (packed with critique, fear, negativity and self-doubt). By constantly practicing the concepts, exercises and tools in this book, your Conscious Mind will be open to the positivity of your Higher Conscious rather than the negativity of your Negative Internal Voice.

Your Conscious Mind is not often aware it is being controlled by your Negative Internal Dialogue and also to what extent. Even if you were aware, the negativity is so commonplace in your mind that you forget to tune into the positivity of your Higher Conscious. In reality "Positive Thinking" relates to you training your Conscious Mind to pay attention to your Higher Conscious by constantly reminding it to do so. Affirmations, books, downloads, music, quotes, etc., are all tools and techniques you can use to keep the flow of positivity running and to help remind your Conscious Mind to focus on the positive Higher Conscious.

What is imperative to understand and remember, is that from a psychological point of view, your mind has *both* facets to it. We are wired that way by nature, and it is essential for our survival that our minds are made up as they are. In an optimal way of thinking, we naturally find a balance between positive and negative. If we were 100% positive all the time, we would maybe be a little oblivious to the dangers of the world and would always end up in a compromised situation because of our naivety. If we were 100% negative all the time, then maybe we would self-destruct with inertia, fear and worry. Our minds were designed to provide us with the best way forward with regards to survival as a species, the problems arise when individually we have an imbalance and the negative thoughts start to overtake the positive ones, and create real problems for us as individuals. Even if you are an uber-confident individual, you *will* have negative thoughts at some point, so there's no point lamenting that fact. It's just becomes a question of dealing with the negativity when it arises and making sure it is not debilitating, long-lasting or fatal.

The key here is to control the negativity so it doesn't create your life experiences to be fear producing and doesn't hinder you from growing and expanding as an individual. If you have become an expert at listening to your Negative Internal Dialogue/Voice, you need to now become an expert at listening to your Higher Conscious. Once you can do that, your fears and worries will dissipate, and for you more realistic choices will be possible.

In summary:

CONTROLLING NEGATIVITY > LISTENING TO YOUR HIGHER CONSCIOUS > GROWTH AND EXPANSION AS AN INDIVIDUAL > NO MORE FEARS AND WORRIES > REALISTIC CHOICES

It can be said that what happens to you is a direct correlation between how you think and what your outcomes are. When you listen to your Higher Conscious good/positive things happen to you, and when you listen to your Negative Internal Voice, bad/negative things happen to you. When your Subconscious Mind receives input from your Conscious Mind, it carries out that input by connecting it internally to your body, your emotions, your intellect and your feelings. So when your Subconscious Mind hears expressions like "I am weak", "I am undeserving", "I am unworthy", "I am useless", it connects those thoughts to your body and makes you become physically weaker and more apathetic as a person. It connects to your emotions and feelings and makes you feel desperate, depressed and helpless. It connects to your intellect and leads you to make bad/wrong choices for yourself. In other words, you become consumed with negativity on *every* level.

When your Subconscious Mind hears positive affirmations and expressions such as, "I am strong", "I am deserving", "I am worthy", "I am useful", then likewise, it connects those thoughts to your body and makes you become physically stronger and more energetic. It connects to your emotions and feelings and makes you feel confident and self-assured. It connects to your intellect and leads you to make better, more optimal choices for yourself. So in this instance, you become consumed with positive energy on *every* level.

This way of thinking connects you to your environment on another level, whereby you also attract what you give out.

This positive energy of your Subconscious Mind enables you to bring back exactly what you have "asked for" from your environment. If you send out negative signals and vibes, then the world around you conspires and obliges what you send out and delivers all sorts of negative things back to you. As human beings, we also work on a subconscious level, picking up signals from others and sending them out in return. We have a "transmitter" and "receiver" system that we are not always consciously aware of. A simple example of this can be observed in the following behavioral examples:-

- If a person smiles and says "good morning" to you, chances are, you will smile back and also acknowledge their greeting.

- If a person looks at you in an aggressive manner and is rude to you, then chances are you will reciprocate what you have just experienced.

In the above examples, your "receiver" picks up the signals from the world around you and reciprocates the signals it has just received. On the same token, your "transmitter" works in the same way:

— If you smile and say "good morning" to another person, chances are, he/she will smile back and also acknowledge your greeting.

- If you look at a person in an aggressive manner and are rude to him/ her, then chances are he/she will reciprocate what they have just experienced.

In the above two examples, your "transmitter" has sent out a signal to the world around you which has been 'picked up' and sent back to you. Although these are simple examples they show how, many times, we are all reactive to our environment and "attract" what we send out.

Just to reiterate: *If you send out negative signals and vibes, then that negative energy will return to you in the form of people avoiding you, you never achieving your goals, you feeling helpless in your life, and you feeling powerless to accomplish any of your desires.*

If you send out positive energy, your environment obliges your Subconscious Mind and delivers back to you all manner of positive things. Other people will have respect for you and your ideals, your goals will be achieved, you will feel hopeful and more optimistic in your life, and you will feel stronger and more powerful as you chase your desires.

If you send out negative energy, you will attract negative energy. If you send out positive energy, you will attract positive energy.

Just as your Subconscious Mind does not judge, neither does The Law of Attraction.

Many things have been said and written about *The Law of Attraction*, and the 'Universal Energy' it is based on. Many everyday sayings are based on this concept: "You get what you give out", "It's a 'you reap what you sow' world", "What goes around comes around", "Like attracts Like", and so on. It's a concept based on 'getting back what you give out' basically. In some more religious beliefs and spiritual ideologies, it can be looked on as 'Karma':

Karma ~n. (in Hinduism and Buddhism) the sum of a person's actions in this and previous lives, seen as affecting their future fate. – ORIGIN Sanskrit, 'action, effect, fate'.

Oxford English Dictionary

The Law of Attraction

"Grateful souls focus on the happiness and abundance present in their lives and this in turn attracts more abundance and joy towards them."

Stephen Richard

As mentioned, it is the belief that "like attracts like" and that by using our energy and focusing on positive thoughts, we can bring about positive results into our lives (the same can of course be said in the negative sense).

This belief is based on the concept that we are made from "pure energy" both in body and thought, and that 'like energy attracts like energy'. On a psychological level, it can be said "the action of the Mind plants that nucleus, which, if allowed to grow undisturbed, will eventually attract to itself all the conditions necessary for its manifestation in outward visible form." (Thomas Troward). If we truly believe in something, then the energy we create from that belief will espouse it to become our eventual reality.

Some people may have trouble accepting or understanding a 'Universal Energy'; even if you are like that, it shouldn't hinder you from being able to tap into your Higher Conscious. However, if you can see yourself connected to something bigger – A Force of Nature/Universal Energy – you no longer need to feel alone and powerless. Your strength becomes highly magnified, and slowly, your fears and worries start to diminish as you realise you are a part of a much bigger and more powerful picture.

When you learn to trust yourself, your Subconscious Mind always manages to connect you with what you are looking for. Sometimes things may seem 'miraculous' in the way they appear to us in our lives, but the reality is, is that it's our desires, ability to trust ourselves and the power of our subconscious that can bring our goals to fruition and make them become our reality.

When you start trusting yourself and you start acting from a true sense of belief, it's amazing the level of strength and power you receive from your thoughts. Things that may have seemed coincidental to you, may have happened because the energy in you and the energy in your environment, simultaneously transpired to make those things happen.

The key is to start listening to the messages that your Subconscious Mind is telling you. Your subconscious clearly picks up signals and information that you are unaware of, or it may contain information that you have 'forgotten' about. Sometimes you need to not let your Conscious Mind interfere, but to just let your subconscious lead you to where you need to be. Have you noticed that you may get your most inspiring ideas when you are just taking it easy and not focusing on a task that needs some sort of a solution … Or that sometimes information and answers come to you when you are *not* actively looking for them, and least expect them? That is your Subconscious Mind at work, giving you the answers and solutions that you need when you sometimes struggle to find them *consciously.*

Once you start to develop your ability to trust yourself, you will be able to let your Subconscious Mind guide you to where you need to be in life. Many times, your Conscious Mind can be over analytical or too rational, and can stop you from doing what you need to be doing by being too restrictive. If you can learn to believe in your subconscious, then sometimes "random" ideas may not really be that random, and your thoughts will be able to move from being restrictive, to being expansive.

If you have a problem in your life, then stop trying to actively find a solution by thinking or worrying about it. Once you learn not to overthink something, the answers to your problem become much more apparent. Your subconscious takes over and leads you in the direction you need to be heading. The solutions that come to you, may be when you least expect it-when you are relaxing or when you are sleeping for example. Sometimes your answers may appear to you in your dreams; you just need to be able to learn to interpret them and understand how their meanings will ultimately be able to help you. Again, your dreams represent your Subconscious Mind at work, whereby it creates vivid images and scenarios which in themselves provide you with what you need to know and the resolutions that you are looking for.

When you are angry and upset about something, your emotions and feelings of hurt take over, and it becomes difficult for you to tune into your Higher Conscious. Aligning yourself to your higher thought processes becomes difficult, as does drawing on the positive energy that is above and all around you. When you stay calm and centered, it becomes much easier to let the positive energy flow through you, and you can then tap into the positive power and energy around you and lose any feelings of anger, fear and upset.

(See the diagram below)

Universal Energy

I

Higher Conscious

I

Conscious Mind

I

Subconscious Mind

If you are angry and upset, how do you get back into a place of being calm and centered so that you can think from your Higher Conscious and tap into the positive Universal Energy that is abundant all-around you?

The two main areas that can make you the most angry and upset, usually relate to relationships and work. For example, if

259

you have a job interview for a job that you really want, your anxiety and stress levels may begin to build. The negativity in your mind begins to take over and you begin to fret, worry and over-emphasize the importance of the job. You may even get paralyzed by fear at the thought of not getting the job. It is important to realign your thoughts and to get back to being calm and centered. By using the techniques you have learned thus far, it will help you to reach these psychological objectives.

Start by repeating your Positive Affirmations; se the Positive Vocabulary you have practiced to put your situation into perspective. Make sure your immediate surroundings are calming and conducive in helping you to tap into your inner source of energy and power; the place within you where you feel calm and secure. Focus on the reality that it is just as easy to think in a positive manner as it is to think in a negative manner, and you can emphasize this by using positive self-talk techniques.

You can say to yourself:

"Although this interview and job are important to me, it is NOT the be all and end all of my existence. If it is meant to be I will get this job, but if it isn't, then something better WILL come my way. I can let my Subconscious Mind take over and find the solutions I need while I keep calm and relaxed about how things will turn out. Everything will work out for me how it is supposed to, and whatever happens, it will be another life experience for me to learn from. In reality, I have nothing to fear, stress or worry over."

It is important that your body and mind work in unison to help you feel fully calm and relaxed about your situation. If you keep repeating positive affirmations and calming words to reflect the truth of your situation, your body will follow your mind and you will feel more relaxed and less tense physically also. Each positive sentence and affirmation draws you closer to feeling calmer and more centered. Once you understand that the outcome is out of your control and that you have done your best, you understand that you can let go. There is nothing to worry over or fear.

Sometimes this process of feeling calm and centered may be difficult, so just find a quiet place without any distractions, so you can relax and 'zone out' until you manage to feel better. Relaxing music can help you align yourself better and quicker. It can set the mood for you and also drown out any superfluous/extraneous noise, and at the same time, this will slowly condition you to relax and draw on your inner strength the moment the music starts playing.

As mentioned, your problems may relate to your relationship and not an interview or a job for example. How would you then cope?

It all comes down to how you perceive a relationship to be and what your expectations are. If a relationship for you means constantly calling and checking up on each other, being together all the time so your partner doesn't leave you, being mistrusting of other people and your partner, then on many levels you are courting the very negativity you are trying to avoid from happening. Although you may love your partner wholeheartedly, it is important to remember that he/she is an individual who is not your possession. It is this ideology that creates jealousy, mistrust and possessiveness in a relationship. Your partner should be free to express himself/herself without fear or prejudice, and at the same time, you should both provide each other with care, love and nurture to help each other grow and become fulfilled.

* Larry loved his wife and wanted to do everything for her in his efforts to keep her. He would try to pander to her every whim and at the same time, he would be very mistrusting of other people in his life and keep them at arm's length. He had very few friends and found it difficult to share his time and emotions with people. Paradoxically, he tried to stop his wife from going out while he at the same time went out as much as he could with his colleagues after work. He didn't like the

idea of his wife talking to other men, and tried to control her in his efforts to keep her from going out. This caused a huge amount of resentment from his wife which was directed towards him both directly and indirectly. He would also track her movements constantly and would also check her telephone and emails whenever he could. This obsessive fear he had in regard to losing his wife meant he did the very things he *shouldn't have done* in his efforts of trying to please her. The further she drifted away from him, the harder he tried to cling on to her and the more possessive he became. In the end, his behaviour became too much for his wife to bear, and eventually she filed for divorce on the grounds of unreasonable behavior.

If you find yourself behaving in a similar manner to Larry, it is important to refocus and realign your thinking, because if you don't, then as in the above example, you will *attract* the very thing that you fear.

You need to think in a different manner and focus on not inviting into your life the very things you are frightened of. You cannot control other people or their actions, you can only control yourself, your actions, your behaviour and your responses. A more optimal way for you to think is like this:

"My partner is not *everything* to me in my life. I love him/her dearly and if we are 'meant to be' then everything will work out for us as I hope it will. I cannot control his/her behavior, I can only focus on myself and do my best to make the relationship work. If it does not work out, then so be it. I gave my all and did my best. I believe in myself and trust in my Subconscious Mind to create the perfect relationship for me. I can relax in the knowledge that everything is as it should be in my life. I am fulfilled, my life consists of many enriched areas, and I know deep down that whatever happens to me I have nothing to worry about and nothing to fear …"

Whatever situation you find yourself stressing over, by learning to believe in and trust in yourself, and by trusting in an outside Force of Nature/Universal Energy, you will accomplish what needs to be done in your life. Sometimes people, situations and circumstances are all drawn together with an indefatigable energy out of your control, which results in something great happening in your life.

FOCUS CONSISTENTLY AND CONSCIOUSLY ON THE SPIRITUAL PART OF YOURSELF. THIS WILL LEAD YOU TO EXPERIENCE HAPPINESS, CONTENTMENT AND A FEELING OF ONENESS IN YOUR LIFE.

It is not easy to constantly strive to train your Conscious Mind to listen to the lessons provided by your Higher Conscious. Day-to-day difficulties and any negativity in your mind may hinder your progress at times, but the key is to keep persevering and be consistent in your efforts to tune into your Higher Conscious.

Every day try to incorporate some time to focus on your Higher Conscious using various tools you have now incorporated into your way of thinking: affirmations, reading positive books/listening to audio books, listening to calming music, or whatever else that works best for you. Try to do this in the morning because it sets up the day ahead and also, before you go to sleep, try instructing your Higher Conscious to find solutions to the problems which you may be encountering in your life. Remember, your Subconscious Mind will also help you by going to work once you fall asleep.

It is important for you to understand that your Higher Conscious is the place that influences every other area of your life. It is from this area of your higher being, that you create value in wherever you choose to go, or in whatever you choose to do. It is from this higher plane that you enhance the quality of your relationships in your life, both with your external world and with your inner self. These relationships may include your partner, your colleagues/clients, your family, your friends, your levels of contribution, your levels of personal growth, and so forth.

When you attain a developed and heightened Higher Conscious, the *loving* and *positive* energy that you can tap into will then be able to flow into every area of your life. As the term "Higher Conscious" suggests, it is a higher level of being that you should aim to reach in your life.

It is important that you remain altruistic and contribute to the lives of others. This enables you to reach your higher self, and the motivation for you is that it infuses you with a greater sense of purpose and energy. If you can contribute to something that you truly believe in, then the rewards for you are even greater. You will feel a deeper sense of satisfaction and a greater sense of oneness together with a heightened Higher Conscious.

When you think of your life on a higher level, it takes on a meaning beyond that of the mere physical. These "metaphysical" thoughts provide you with a deeper understanding of how the world truly works and the role that you play in it. This enables you to create greater trust in yourself and greater trust in the world around you. This in turn will allay all your fears, concerns and difficulties. These concepts together with the others in this book may take you a lifetime to practice, but the reality is that they will provide you with direction, meaning and purpose throughout your life. As mentioned earlier, being spiritual does not have a religious connotation, but whether or not you are, these metaphysical thoughts and concepts will be of equal worth to you.

* **Metaphysics** ~**n.** philosophy concerned with abstract ideas such as the nature of existence, truth and knowledge.

(Oxford English Dictionary)

When you learn to start thinking from a higher place, you learn to incorporate self-actualization, self-integration and self-realization into your existence. These can all release you from past conditioning, past struggles and help to resolve negative conflicts within you. The benefits being that you reawaken your creative awareness and develop your loving nature.

The central theme on a psychological level for you is:

I WANT TO BE INDEPENDENT + SELF-SUFFICIENT AND I DON'T NEED TO BE TAKEN CARE OF BY ANYONE.

Certain practices can help you develop your Higher Conscious: hypnotherapy, psychotherapy and visualization for example. Guided Visualization Techniques help you to relax both your body and mind as you listen to instructions to help you. These techniques help you to use the power of your imagination to see your life as it would be seen if you only listened to your Higher Conscious. Usually, your imagination is plugged into your Negative Internal Thinking and the only images that you can conjure up are filled with fear, stress and worry. With Guided Visualization Techniques you can learn to push aside the negativity which permeates your everyday thinking and tune into mental images and pictures that you have not imagined or seen before. The understanding this creates for you with the use of imagery can be truly overwhelming. Both positive and negative images can be beneficial. From the negatives the valuable lessons you can learn relate to insights that you may have been avoiding and hiding from.

It's imperative that you try Visualization because the Mind can create more easily what it can see. If however you struggle to practice the art of Visualization, then don't be perturbed, because you can use other tools such as Affirmations, Meditation or other Relaxation Techniques to help you reach your higher being and get in touch with your Higher Conscious.

To help you visualize, you can practice by listening to audio books or listening to downloads that can help you to focus on the images and visuals needed to help create the right environment for your higher self. An example of practicing a Visualization Technique is as follows:

Visualization Technique

- Close your eyes and keep them closed throughout the visualization process.

- Take a deep breath in then exhale slowly.

- Repeat the deep breathing until you feel more and more relaxed.

- Relax your muscles from top to toe, until you can feel all the tension leaving your body.

- Think of a specific goal that you have in your life (one that you have struggled to attain up until now).

- Imagine approaching your goal with no apprehension or fear in your mind.

- Approach your goal with a renewed sense of power and confidence in yourself and in your abilities.

- Imagine what you would be doing if you had no fear.

- See yourself: What would you be doing next if nothing could hold you back?

- How are you relating to the people around you in your heightened confident state?

- How are other people relating to you?

- Enjoy your sense of power and feel your ability to contribute and be more loving to your surroundings.

- Understand that this feeling is always a part of you.

- Know that it is within your capability to move forwards in your life with the confidence and power that you can feel.

- See yourself actualizing your goal: with your confidence; with your power; with your love; with your contribution.

- After you have visualized *actualizing* your goal, slowly bring yourself back to the room you are in.

- Know that the power is available to you at any time … As soon as you act towards achieving your goal, the power will come forward from within you.

- Feel yourself in your chair, be present and aware of yourself in your room, and when you are ready, open your eyes.

- Feel and know that the confidence and power you need is within you, waiting to be drawn upon whenever you require.

When you learn to remove the apprehension and fear that blight your thoughts, you will have more confidence in being able to achieve your goals and you will also feel an abundance of love. Once fear is removed from your world, you will be left with the realization that your environment really is a beautiful place, and you will also have an increased desire to help others and be more altruistic. Tuning into your Higher Conscious will help you find your way in life, it will illuminate the path ahead for you and it will help you to see what you are striving for.

What can Visualization help you with?

You can find answers to questions about the meaning and purpose of your life. You can clarify your life goals. You can reveal important truths that you are denying yourself or blocking from your mind. You can use these applications to provide incredible insights into your life. In fact, because Visualization is so powerful, it can be used as a valuable tool by coaches, lecturers, therapists *and by you*, to tap into your inner power.

The way you think and the way you behave *is* a choice - always remember that! Whether or not you choose to use the tools and techniques you have thus far learned will resonate in the life that you live and the outcomes that result for you. Always strive to connect to and think with your Higher Conscious.

"There is no coming to consciousness without pain. People will do anything, no matter how absurd, in order to avoid facing their own soul. One does not become enlightened by imagining figures of light, but by making the darkness conscious".

C. G. Jung

REMEMBER: YOU HAVE THE POWER TO ATTRACT AND TO CHOOSE POSITIVE OVER NEGATIVE

Negative Thought	Higher Conscious Thought
I need	I love
I repel	I attract
I take	I give
I control	I trust
I am lacking	I am abundant
I am tense	I am relaxed
I am in turmoil	I am at peace
I am blocked	I am creative
I am weak	I am strong
I am lonely	I have friends & family
I am helpless	I am helpful
I am empty	I am fulfilled
I am melancholic	I am joyful

I am insensitive	I am nurturing
I am dissatisfied	I am content
I am resentful	I am forgiving
I am filled with self-doubt	I am confident
I am vulnerable	I am protected
I am confused	I am filled with clarity
I am bored	I am excited
I am unappreciative	I am appreciative
I am fearful	I am fearless

CHAPTER TWELVE:

ATTAINING INNER PEACE

"Peace is not a result inside us from everything around us. Peace is not submissive nor passive. On the contrary, peace is an overwhelming force which comes from within us, disrespectful of everything around us, a firm coalition of spirit and soul standing against all the unrest that abounds."

C. Joybell C.

You may have heard the term "Inner Peace" being used and wondered exactly what it is. Simply put, it is the feeling of having "Peace of Mind" and having a sense of calmness both mentally and spiritually. It relates to you having enough knowledge and understanding to keep you feeling strong in the face of adversity and through difficult times. "Inner Peace/Peace of Mind" are expressions that are used to indicate that you are balanced and that your mindset and outlook are healthy as opposed to feeling anxious, stressed or worried. Inner Peace/Peace of Mind are often inter-connected to feelings of bliss, contentment and happiness.

Inner Peace, calmness and serenity are descriptions of an emotional or mental disposition that are free from the effects of negativity, stress and worry. In Western cultures, we are adopting more and more the teachings of other cultures, especially of those in the Far East, whereby Inner Peace is considered a state of consciousness or enlightenment. These concepts may be cultivated further by various forms of training such as meditation, prayer and yoga, for example. Finding inner peace is often associated to the teachings of Buddhism and Hinduism and the spiritual practices refer to this inner peace as an experience of "knowing oneself".

"The question of real, lasting world peace concerns human beings, so basic human feelings are also at its roots. Through inner peace, genuine World peace can be achieved. In this the importance of individual responsibility is quite clear; an atmosphere of peace must first be created within ourselves, then gradually expanded to include our families, our communities, and ultimately the whole planet".

Tenzin Gyatso, Dalai Lama

When you feel at peace with your surroundings and within yourself, this level of consciousness/ enlightenment means that you have full understanding and comprehension of the situations that you find yourself in throughout your life. You just need to bear in mind that to attain this level of understanding about who you are and your role in the world, you just need diligence and patience:

ATTAINING INNER PEACE AND ENLIGHTENMENT IS A PROCESS.

How would you go about achieving Inner Peace and Enlightenment in your life?

Now that you understand being calm and peaceful relates to thinking in the Higher Conscious, it is important that you know how to practice the necessary steps needed in order to learn and think from this higher level of consciousness.

1) – **Be calm and patient at all times**: Remember that feelings of being at peace with yourself and your surroundings develop over time. Fluctuations will occur at different stages in your life, so just focus on being patient when it is necessary.

2) – **Replenish and soothe your mind**:

a) Free yourself of stresses and worry - Find a quiet location so that you can just sit peacefully and empty your mind of all thought until you feel relaxed.

b) Rest frequently - Find a comfortable place where you can meditate, relax, take a nap or just unwind, away from everyone and everything.

3) – **Make everything as simple as possible**: Try not to rush around and do everything at once. On the same token, try not to overcomplicate things in your life. Keep things simple and do things in good time.

4) – **Live in the moment**: Try to think less about the past or future. Don't stress over what has already happened or what may never happen. Think about what you are doing as you are doing it so that you can focus all your energies on the task at hand.

5) – **Don't prejudge**: It is important that you learn to let go of biases and expectations that you hold on to. By doing this, you become much more open to the experiences that your life has to offer.

6) – **Be happy and positive**: Keep on a positive track in your life by satisfying your desires and by taking the time out to do the things that make you happy.

7) – **Have more pride**: There is only one you, so have more pride in your individuality. After all, you are who you are, so be proud of it.

8) – **Feel more contentment in your life**: It is imperative that you find contentment in who you are, where you find yourself in life, and in what you are doing. This will help you to acknowledge the positives that are in your life.

9) – **Take more responsibility for your actions**: Don't live in denial! It's important that you learn to rectify any errors or hurt that you may have caused other people (if this is possible). Otherwise, learn to let go of any stresses that affect you by owning up to what you do and how you behave.

10) – **Be a good person**: By being courteous, kind and pleasant, the benefits are two-fold; Not only do other people benefit from your behaviour, but you are also left with a deep-rooted sense of joy and satisfaction.

11) – **Appreciate the beauty around you**: Don't look for negatives in your world, learn to develop your ability to notice and see the beauty in yourself, everyone else and everything else that you come across on a daily basis.

12) – **Focus on Love**: Not in a flippant way, but learn to appreciate the spirit of other people, and let love be your guiding light and illuminator in your life.

13) – **Take your time over things**: Don't be busy rushing from place to place all the time. By being calmer and more observant, you learn to enjoy and experience your life and also your surroundings in a better way.

14) – **Take it easy and relax**: It is important for you to know that you need to do things for yourself, that you need to take more time out for yourself and stop ignoring your needs.

15) – **Be more private**: Stop creating unnecessary dramas in your life. Learn to keep things to yourself and focus more on your inner needs without the interference of other people.

16) – **Be content and satisfied with your life**: Learn to find contentment in your work, your relationship and with everything else in your life, because contentment is the *most important* aspect of attaining Inner peace. By being contented you will benefit by being more joyful and satisfied in your life.

17) – **List as many reasons as you can about why you love yourself**: This is a very useful tool for you for the times in your life when you are feeling a little low. Go over your attributes to help you remember the good aspects about who you are and what you have achieved.

18) – **Work out what sort of environment you want to live in**: You will feel a lot better and a lot calmer once you work out the type of world you want to live in, and the sort of surroundings you want to find yourself in. The objective of this is to help you find out where you can feel most relaxed to enable you to tune into your Higher Conscious.

19) – **Live a healthier lifestyle**: Although this sounds very clichéd, it really makes a difference to your mood depending on what you choose to nourish yourself with. To boost your physical and emotional energy, eat plenty of fresh fruit and vegetables and cut out sugars, fats and pre-prepared foods. Also cut down on caffeine and alcohol which also affect your mood and sleep patterns. Being healthy is key to calmness and feeling more relaxed.

20) – **Work out the reasons why you want to find Inner Peace**: Find a quiet place so that you can work out why you feel you need to have more calm and peace in your life. Is your life full of drama? Do you continually choose the 'wrong' people to associate yourself with? Do you naturally stress over everything that is happening to you? Working out your feelings and the decisions that you need to make will help you achieve your goals.

21) – **Be more optimistic**: By being optimistic, you actually learn to look forward to things in your life. You only have one shot at being who you are and living the life you live, so you owe it to yourself to do the best you can and to be the best person that you can be. By being optimistic you become more open to the opportunities and possibilities that your life has to offer, and by living this way, your aim of attaining Inner Peace will truly be accomplished.

In reality, until you learn to deal properly with the external stressors in your life, your life will remain complicated and you will continue to suffer from inner turmoil which will then be projected by you back onto the world around you. By following the steps above, you will slowly be able to rid yourself of the difficulties that blight your existence. You will find inner peace when the inner turmoil in you ends. You need to stop looking outside yourself for solutions to your problems, and instead you need to turn your attentions and focuses inwards to 'make peace' with your own experiences of life. Although you may find this concept difficult to start with, once you realise you need to move your attention and focus, the results will be astounding. Many inner conflicts will be healed, you will feel a lot calmer and you will gain deeper clarity of what is truly happening in your life.

"Making the darkness Conscious"

As Jung implied, you may be an expert at denying what happens to you in your life. If you have any negative habits that don't serve you well, such as being envious/jealous, being judgmental, having compulsive behaviors, desperately wanting to be "needed" by others, and so on, then these negative behaviour patterns can all be traced back to a root problem which more often than not is based on expectations and feelings that you are avoiding.

If you hide or deny these root problems, then they just thrive in your psyche and leave you with a profound sense of fear and an inability to unconsciously drive your behaviour in the correct manner. Once you learn to illuminate the root causes of your negative behaviour patterns by becoming *aware* of them, then you begin to understand how you operate, and this leads you to making more optimal choices. This will equate to: no more angst, no more conflict, no more confusion, no more difficulty and no more turmoil. *Result = Inner Peace*.

ROOT PROBLEMS > IRRATIONAL BEHAVIOURS AND NEGATIVE FEELINGS.

AWARENESS OF ROOT PROBLEMS > BETTER UNDERSTANDING > BETTER CHOICES > NO MORE NEGATIVITY = INNER PEACE.

Unearthing your deeper root causes and problems may be difficult and painful, but each revelation will lead you away from the negativity and pattern of bad choices that you continually make, and you will eventually be led to a simpler and more conscious level of being. This realization will lead you away from difficulty and neurotic behaviors. What results is an end to your suffering and a feeling of freedom and release, whereby you become consciously more open to amazement, creativity, joy and happiness.

Finding out who you are

Trying to find out what your deeper motivations and what your root problems are requires courage and openness on your part. Whether you choose to work alone, or with the help of a counsellor/therapist, you need to be willing and prepared to be:

- Honest about who you are and what you are doing.

- Ready to feel some pain, but not let it debilitate you.

- Ready to let go of past negativity and change for the better.

- Able to contemplate a new kind of 'inner being', one which is not hindered by confusion, distress and turmoil.

- Content, happy, peaceful and more relaxed.

When you can accept the reality of who you *are* and who you strive *to be*, then you are ready to explore yourself. After all, self-improvement is one of the best and most compassionate things that you can ever do for yourself. The steps mentioned earlier will help you find the inner peace that you are looking for. If you want to delve deeper into your mind and be in better control, then remember these five key points:

1) When you are faced with a 'trigger': Instead of behaving in your usual manner, stop, re-focus, think about what is happening and breathe deeply, so that you begin to feel in control of the situation.

2) Be Aware of: Your thought patterns, your emotions and the bodily sensations that you are feeling. Don't lose control of yourself, just be inquisitive and ask yourself: "What am I thinking? What are the emotions and physical sensations that I am currently experiencing? What is the energy behind my thoughts and feelings?" When you can ask these questions, you allow yourself to become familiar with your actions, habits and thoughts, so that *they* no longer control you.

3) Find the most caring and loving place inside you: This is your natural caring and nurturing self that comes to the fore when you are close to the people that you love the most. Use these powerful expressions of love on yourself so that you can heal any hurt, pain or turmoil that is inside you.

4) Learn to repeat: It is important that you learn to develop your 'coping strategies' so that every time you are struggling to cope, you can draw on the techniques and tools you have thus far learned to help you get through your most difficult times. Remember that emotional exercise is just like physical exercise, you have to keep repeating what you do to get results.

5) Move ahead when the time is right: When you are ready, move forwards in the best way possible that supports you as you wish to be. Make sure you have the clarity to see your life as optimally as you possibly can. Make sure your thoughts and actions provide you and others with happiness, and make sure that you focus on your emotional and physical wellbeing.

How would you implement a calmer way of being into your life?

I) Relationship Conflicts

This is probably the major area of conflict and difficulty for most people, because after all, many people have problems in maintaining successful relationships. Divorce is at an all-time high, and for many people, it is common place to have multiple dates, multiple relationships or even failed relationship after failed relationship.

A break-up can't always be the other person's fault, and you can't always end up choosing 'the wrong type' because by implying so, you absolve yourself of all responsibility from the failed relationship; After all, this implies that you see your break-ups as being *the other person's* fault because *they* are of the 'wrong type'.

Do you have the tendency to blame the other person for the difficulties in your relationships? Is it difficult for you to find fault in your own behaviour, yet you have no trouble seeing and pointing out the other person's 'faults'? Do you get angry at the way the other person in your relationship speaks or behaves?

If these questions apply to you and you have answered in the affirmative, then you are behaving in a child-like way with no responsibility for *your* role in the relationship. Your habitual behaviour of "passing the buck" has meant that you are playing the "if only" game with yourself: "If only my partner would change I would be happier. If only my partner were more understanding of *me*, then things would be so much better. If only my partner made me happier, I wouldn't do what I do…"

When you think like this and say these things to yourself, you will never be happy or solve your problems because your mindset is wrong. It is wrong because you are making **your** peace of mind dependent on factors out of your control, i.e. what **other** people say and do.

If your relationships are always problematic and stressful, then you need to start by 'making peace' with your own reactions. Your attentions should be directed inwards to meet your deep-rooted fears, frustrations and other triggers in a positive manner. You may not like the answers that you find, but by firstly realising and accepting who *you* are, you will then be on the road to finding more calm and peace in your life. Also rather importantly, by seeing *your* role in the conflict, it will help you to unlock the possibility of finding better and more compassionate solutions in the future. Remember:

EVERYTHING IN A RELATIONSHIP IS 50 – 50, BOTH THE CONFLICTS AND THE SOLUTIONS, SO BE RESPONSIBLE FOR YOUR 50%

II) Holding on to Anger

Imagine carrying around anger with you for a long time. For weeks, for months or for years even. To keep this anger alive, you must constantly re-live what happened in the past and tell yourself all the things that should or should not have happened at that point. You are consumed with angst and rage every time you think of the situation again or are faced with other triggers that remind you of the anger inducing memories. Living in this state of mind is hardly beneficial for you, both in terms of your psychological or physical welfare.

Every time you re-live past events, the negative thoughts that they invoke keep you stuck at the points of what happened to you in the past. If you truly want to release yourself from them, you need to let them go. You can do this by breaking them down into two smaller elements- your thoughts and your physical sensations. Despite the pain that you may feel, understand your role in the event, and then forgive yourself for the negative experience that has been affecting you and making you angry. You couldn't help feeling the way you did at the time, but you need to draw a line under the event and move forwards with your life, leaving the anger where it belongs, in the past. Whoever hurt you is no longer your responsibility, but by holding onto the anger, you let them still have some control over you. *When you let go of the anger, they have no more influence over you.*

This process does not condone what happened to you, and in reality does not even concern the other person/s. The real focal point about past anger or hurt relates to the choice that *you* have. Do you choose to continue holding on to anger which will affect you mentally and physically, or do you choose to move forwards in your life by forgiving yourself and creating happiness and peace of mind?

III) Addictions and Bad Habits

It is important for you to realise that the bad and negative habits that you have, mask a deeper, unexplored emotion, usually connected to feelings of sorrow or fear. Without realising it, these challenging habits that you perpetuate follow a compulsive pattern that involves what you do physically and how you think mentally. This pattern then manifests itself in your actions, emotions, feelings and in your thinking. If you find yourself lost in neurotic thoughts, and always feel apprehensive and anxious about what is happening in your life, or if you drink, smoke or take other drugs excessively, then all these may be an attempt by you to escape from any deep-rooted sorrow or fear that is the real cause of why you behave the way you do.

If you want to try and control your addictions and compulsions, and to bring an element of calmness and peace into your inner world, then every time you feel the urge to carry out a detrimental 'habit', it is vital that you stop, re-focus and move your thoughts towards the feelings that you have been trying to avoid. Your bad habits are just the way you have conditioned yourself to cope with whatever is stressing you on a deeper level. You need to learn how to *change your habits* so that you can free yourself from your addictions and neurotic repetitions.

Tips for changing habits from bad to good

1) – Focus on one habit at a time: Changing habits is notoriously difficult, so keep it simple and only focus on one habit at a time.

2) – Start with small changes: Because changing bad habits is not easy, it is vital you focus on small changes rather than large ones which you may find too difficult to start with.

3) – Take up a one month challenge: It takes roughly one month to change a habit. Although this may vary from person to person and habit to habit, starting with a one month challenge is attainable for you if you are focused and consistent. Different studies have been written about how long it takes to create a new habit, anything from twenty-one days to two months. A good beginning is to start and continue with something new for one month.

4) – Make a note of what you want to achieve: It is important that you write down your commitment to change so that you can *see* your intentions. Sign and date it also for added confirmation.

5) – Draw up a Plan: Write down a plan also stating your motivational reasons for wanting to change. Also include ways that will enable you to achieve success such as, overcoming obstacles, a support network and facing any triggers that you may encounter.

6) – Know your motivational reasons: In your plan make it clear *why* you are creating this change and the benefits that will result for you. Also, Make sure your motivations are good and sustainable.

7) – Create a start date: This gives your plan an air of importance and significance and it will also help you to prepare for it by building up anticipation and excitement. At the same time, tell as many people as you can about what you are planning to do.

8) – List your obstacles: Make note of anything that may stop you or that already has stopped you if you have tried to do it before. After listing your obstacles, write down how you plan to overcome them. Preparation is key, so write down solutions *before* the obstacles occur.

9) – Identify triggers: Have you worked out what triggers your current habit? Most habits have multiple triggers so it is imperative that you identify them all and include them in your plan.

10) – For every trigger identify a positive habit to replace it: After identifying your triggers, do something constructive instead of giving in to the trigger. These positive habits may include exercise, relaxation techniques, meditation, clearing up, reading, organizing, etc.

11) – Create a support system: Write down the people who you can turn to when you have strong urges to give in to your habit. Gaining support from friends and family is really important.

12) – Ask for help when it's needed: Once you have created your support network, don't hold back when you need their help. Know that you will have weak moments, so you will need the help of others to overcome these blips.

13) – Listen to your Higher Conscious: Let your higher-self guide you through the process of change. Anytime your

negative thinking starts up, learn to get past those thoughts with positive affirmations from your Higher Conscious.

14) – Stay Positive: Understand that any low point you go through will be natural and will be followed by a high. Keep repeating positive sentences and quotes to help you get through the down periods.

15) – Create strategies to defeat any urges: Be prepared for any strong urges and understand that these are natural. Know that they are only temporary and that you can defeat them. Urges don't last very long, but they do come in waves of varying degree. Once you see out the wave, the urge *will* go away. Strategies to help include contacting your support network, exercising, going for a walk, relaxation techniques, meditation, listening to music or eating something healthy.

16) – Prepare for negativity: You will encounter people who are negative or who want to sabotage your plans and goals. Be ready for them and confront them if need be. If people don't support you, then you should avoid them, plain and simple.

17) – Talk yourself up: Don't be afraid to talk to yourself in an effort to remind you of your goals. Push yourself and encourage yourself with positive sentences and mantras. The best pep talks can come from you.

18) – Create a mantra for yourself: A positive mantra will constantly remind you of what needs to be done. Write it down and repeat it when need be. You can find a mantra that works for you or create one for yourself - "Under no circumstances will I give up", or words to that effect.

19) – Use visualization: We have looked at visualization earlier, but a good use for it is when you want to stop any bad

habits that you have. Picture yourself successfully changing your habits from bad to good. Visualize yourself overcoming any urges and successfully conquering each trigger. *See* yourself carrying out your new habits and giving up your old ones for good.

20) – Reward yourself: Create milestones for yourself in your plan, and at each successful accomplishment reward yourself. This helps you to remain positive and focus on the next step you need to reach.

21) – Deal with one urge at a time: When you are trying to give up bad behaviors or habits, it really is a question of getting through each urge as it arises. You only need to focus on and overcome the next obstacle (urge).

22) – Break the bond between bad habits and triggers: You must be consistent and realise that there are no exceptions in your efforts to break a bond and form a new one. When faced with a trigger carry out the *new* habit and *not* the old habit. If you fail, then regroup and continue as before.

23) – Rest and Recuperate: Make sure you have the energy to overcome your urges. When you are tired, you feel irritable and therefore more vulnerable to relapse. So focus on plenty of 'R & R' in your first month.

24) – Eat well and drink plenty of water: Bad diets and dehydration leave you feeling irritable and vulnerable also, so make sure your diet and hydration levels are good.

25) – Continue to renew your commitment to change: As often as possible, remind yourself of what you are doing and why. Go over your plan, repeat positive affirmations, repeat your mantra and be prepared for any obstacles and urges.

26) – Be accountable: By continually making your plans and progress public, you have more people to answer to, and as a result you make sure that *failure is not an option*.

27) – Make it hard to fail: Create an environment which makes it more difficult for you to stop your new habit. This way you are more likely to continue with your new habit because failure will have a cost for you/a price to pay.

28) – Avoid people and situations that result in your old habits resurfacing: Whether you want to stop smoking, drinking, eating bad food, taking drugs, or whatever your vice may be, it is important you stay away from your triggers, *especially* during the first month. When you return to the old environment, be prepared for the old urges to also return. It is at these times that you need to be especially strong. Sometimes though, a clean break is required from your triggers and temptations.

29) – Don't give up: If you do fail, work out what went wrong, work out a new plan of action and try again. Refocus and regroup making sure that you avoid feeling guilty at all costs. So long as you learn from failure, it won't count as a failure, but merely a 'stepping stone' on your pathway to success. Once you have reached the level of success you are after, you will feel euphoric and proud in the knowledge that you can achieve what you put your mind to achieving. Long term benefits include feelings of satisfaction, a deeper sense of calmness and a more powerful sense of inner strength and peace of mind.

Whatever is troubling you in your life, the first step to finding inner peace involves you becoming aware of what the deeper problem is. When you focus your energies on resolution, as you can now see, that begins the process of simplifying the problem immediately and you can find long-lasting solutions which will improve the quality of your life. Focus on whatever may be troubling you right now and find solutions using the steps above.

To create the inner calmness and peace that will help you rid yourself of any negative actions and thoughts, you need to focus on being aware of what they are. Very few problems just go away of their own accord. You need to work on them, however hard it may be for you. Being attentive and aware may not be a panacea that rids you of all your negative behaviour patterns, but it is a start to taking you to where you need to be in your life. By implementing this new way of thinking and using the correct tools and techniques, then the calmness, serenity and inner peace that you desire, will follow before long.

"Happiness, true happiness, is an inner quality. It is a state of mind. If your mind is at peace, you are happy. If your mind is at peace, but you have nothing else, you can (still) be happy. If you have everything the world can give – pleasure, possessions, power – but lack peace of mind, you can never be happy."

Dada Vaswani

CHAPTER THIRTEEN:

CONTINUING THE JOURNEY

"Never make a home in a place. Make a home for yourself inside your own head. You'll find what you need to furnish it – memory, friends you can trust, love of learning, and other such things. That way it will go with you wherever you journey."

Tad Williams

Now that you are filled with all sorts of ideas, information, techniques, tools and much more, you are nearing the end of one journey and about to embark on a new one. You are now enlightened when it comes to understanding yourself better, and you have also learned about the following subjects:

- **Facing Your Fears**

- **Going For Your Goals**

- **Empowerment**

- **Are You A Victim?**

- **Positive Thinking**

- **Dealing With The Negatives**

- **Decision Making**

- **Overcoming Emotional Problems**

- **Acceptance And Fulfilment**

- **Kismet And The Power Of Giving**

- **Your Higher Conscious And The Law Of Attraction**

- **Attaining Inner Peace**

What next for you?

Understand that during your down periods and weaker moments as you continue on your journey, this book will always be available for you to pick up and go over the points that will be relevant for you at that particular time in your life. Together with other books, downloads, audio books and the like, you will have a cornucopia of information and ideas on hand to provide you with the 'emotional sustenance' that you'll need to help you move forwards whenever you feel stuck or troubled at a particular point in your life.

Try to control the negative thoughts and dialogue in your mind which sabotage your existence by being critical, disapproving and impatient. This negativity leads to nothing positive in your life, and is just a way of punishing yourself. It also hinders you on your efforts to move forward.

It is important that you pace yourself in the correct manner and don't expect changes to happen overnight. Stay focused because you have the power within you to achieve all your goals, you just need to be calm, diligent and *patient* in your efforts to accomplish them.

Many times in our lives, we have created all the right parameters for success, but where we fail is due to us being impatient, or worse still giving up altogether. Don't give up if you can't see anything happening as quickly as you had anticipated. One reason that you bought this book is because you felt you needed some changes in your life. You needed counselling, you needed coaching and you needed guidance to help you and to keep you on track throughout your journey. Maybe you have been stuck in a rut because of a divorce or because of family problems, or maybe you have reached a crossroads in your life with regard to work or a relationship you're involved in. Whatever challenges you are facing in your life, understand that they are only temporary. Once you have planted the seed for change, it *will* happen at its own pace. You can't rush it. Change will happen organically within you when the time is right. The only thing you need to do is nourish 'the seed of change' that is within you. Nurture it with all the necessary ingredients to help it grow and blossom into something that will flourish within you and benefit you.

BE PATIENT BECAUSE PATIENCE MEANS KNOWING DEEP DOWN THAT SOMETHING GOOD *WILL* EVENTUALLY HAPPEN.

How you continue to live your life will depend on how you view it. Maybe you feel life is just one big learning curve or that your experiences in life all stem from your Higher Conscious. You may even feel that life is only a set of random events that take place because of Fate/Kismet. However you view your life, it is important that you understand *other ways of being* which may be more optimal for you. However you choose to live your life, you have to trust yourself because at some point you may confront intense difficulty, and it is at these points of difficulty that lessons are there to be learned. When you trust in yourself, you become better at learning what needs to be learned in order to overcome difficulties, and you distance yourself from being a victim. Accept that whatever happens to you at any given time in your life, it is an opportunity to learn and grow from.

ALWAYS BE PATIENT BECAUSE LIFE IS AN ONGOING PROCESS OF LEARNING WITH CONTINUAL LESSONS ALONG THE WAY.

Trying to understand what truly makes you happy in your life can be a difficult process. You may have spent hours mulling over different answers, ideas and scenarios in your head, yet the greatest joy life has to offer may simply relate to being able to work out 'what your life is really all about'. *Understanding yourself* and *understanding your world* are gifts that elude most people in their lives. Make sure you are not one of them. Make sure your life has real value and meaning both for yourself and for everyone else that comes into contact with you. Discover the true Secret of Existence and Fulfilment …

… THAT THE JOY OF DISCOVERING *YOURSELF* IS DELIGHTFUL.

The real challenge that you will face as you continue on your life journey, is to stay on the path to your Higher Conscious. As mentioned earlier, trust is important, and it is with this trust that you will be able to work out if you are on the right path in your life. ***Trust how you feel. Trust what you have learned. Trust in yourself.*** **The only guide that you have as you move forwards in your life is *YOU*.** If where you are heading in your life isn't providing you with caring, creativity, contentment, fulfilment, joy, love and satisfaction, then you need to know that you are not heading in the right direction. To work out the best direction you need to be heading in, is not a question of changing everything externally, it is more a question of changing things internally. Internal changes will change your surroundings and therefore will change what happens to you.

BY CHANGING YOURSELF *INTERNALLY*, YOU WILL CHANGE YOUR WORLD *EXTERNALLY*.

As difficult as it may be to turn your focus *inwards*, it is something that needs to be done. The pathways that need changing are within you, primarily the ones in your mind. Of course, once you have aligned your mind to your Higher Conscious, you will feel a new sense of energy and power that will come from your new found understanding. This will mean you will have a huge desire to change others also, and even to try to influence and change the world in some way; but remember, before you can do that, it is *your mind* that has to be changed first.

ONCE *YOU* HAVE CHANGED, YOU CAN THEN HELP CHANGE *OTHERS*.

It is quite common for people to try to help others once they themselves have accomplished a goal in life. That is why so many people who have lost weight want to help others to lose weight. That is why so many people who have suffered loss want to help others cope in their moment of loss. That is why people who have suffered trauma want to help others overcome their traumas. Once you yourself have experienced change, you have the knowledge and power to help others.

When you think of the pathway to your Higher Conscious, think of it as a higher place that you aspire to be. Think of yourself climbing to achieve this optimal place of being and thinking. Although the climb will be tough, you know it will be worth your while to reach the top. From this higher level of being, you will feel much freer and much lighter from the troubles of the world below. The Higher you reach on your level of Consciousness, the more beautiful your life and surroundings will be.

From this higher level of awareness and being, you also become far more compassionate and far less judgmental. You learn to let things go that hurt you, you also learn to let go of anger, bitterness and turmoil. You realise there is no use in holding onto such negativity, because after all, the *only* person that you will hurt with these emotions, is yourself.

This 'higher journey' won't always be easy for you, sometimes it will be difficult to 'rise above' certain situations or triggers, but if you remain focused, you can easily overcome any setbacks by regrouping, refocusing and consolidating what you have thus far learned. It then becomes a question of you being able to move onwards and upwards.

As you aspire to become a better person, with better rationale, better judgement and better experiences of life, you may have to drop certain behaviors and beliefs that have always been a part of you. Even if you attain a sudden epiphany, these sudden insights are the result of everything that has gone on in your life before. Your Subconscious Mind is always at work, and when you least expect it, it will come up with solutions for you. The higher up you reach on your level of self-awareness, the more insights will become apparent to you.

Always remember:

THE HIGHER YOUR LEVEL OF SELF-AWARENESS, THE EASIER YOUR CONSCIOUS MIND LETS GO OF ITS RESISTANCE TO NEW WAYS OF THINKING.

Your Conscious Mind develops more trust in your abilities to overcome any difficulties that life throws at you. However far you are on your ascent to your Higher Conscious, just when you think you have found all the answers, something will happen to you in your life to show you that you haven't.

THERE IS ALWAYS MORE TO LEARN AND EXPERIENCE IS YOUR GREATEST TEACHER.

"A mind that is stretched by a new experience can never go back to its old dimensions."

O. W. Holmes, Jr.

When you think back to your youth, although you had energy, enthusiasm and a *joie de vivre*, you didn't have experience, insight and understanding. As we get older, we trade one set of circumstances for another. Understand that the 'joys of youth' will be replaced with the 'joys of living'. The joys in your life *are* abundant if you choose to see them and choose to accept them. If you can see yourself developing and growing as a person, there is no need for you to hanker for the past at all, because you realise that with age, comes beauty and true understanding of yourself and of your life - "Don't ever complain about getting old, because so many people are denied that privilege!"

Whatever stage of your life you are at, there is still so much awe and excitement in front of you. Sometimes your life-experiences will bring you joy and satisfaction, and sometimes your life-experiences will bring you agony and pain. It is important to remember that on your journey through life, you are not alone: someone, somewhere before you has already felt that pain, and they can help you if you are willing to learn. There are many support systems available for you whenever you are feeling troubled about some aspect of your life: friends, family, groups, counsellors, therapists, books, etc. The network of support *is* available, so there is no need for you to suffer in silence. By doing nothing, nothing happens, therefore, you need to take action and be proactive:

NOTHING WILL WORK FOR YOU UNLESS YOU WORK FOR IT.

Your happiness depends on you being able to use all your powers to their fullest, so for that reason, your happiness should be your goal in life. Be positive about every aspect of your life- Do whatever it takes for you to be involved **100%** in your life: participate, be proactive, take a stand, make a difference, but above all, you need to do *something*.

"Happiness comes from within. It is not dependent on external things or on other people. You become vulnerable and can be easily hurt when your feelings of security and happiness depend on the behaviour and actions of other people. Never give your power to anyone else."

Brian L Weiss

Your happiness can be defined as your ability to laugh, to feel humorous, to feel joyous and to feel light (free of burden). Your happiness can express the ebullience of your Higher Conscious and that of your spiritual side. When you have found that place from within, you will be able to let go of your fears, your vulnerabilities and your worries. What remains is your fluidity based on your inner calm, inner grace and inner compassion.

When you feel like this, you move into being a fully functioning *Adult* operating from a higher level, one which is filled with compassion, filled with joy, filled with love, and free from your child-like desires and behaviors. From this higher level of being, you really do have so much that you can offer your immediate surroundings, and then from there, to the world at large.

All you need is a deeper belief and a strong-willed commitment to push yourself through whatever is holding you back in your life. With a few adjustments to how you live, and the love and power of your Higher Conscious, you can achieve truly great things with your life. Whatever your job is, and whatever your background is, you have the capacity to truly empower yourself and to touch the lives of others in the process.

When you live in the most optimal way possible, you will find yourself moving closer and closer to who you *really are*. What's more, when you finally work out who you are and what the meaning of your life is, you can go anywhere and achieve anything that you desire without anyone ever holding you back again. What you will ultimately find, is that the only person who has ever held you back in your life ... has been *You ...*

"Sometimes the dreams that come true are the dreams you never even knew you had ..."

Alice Sebold